Enjoy ~~~
Serece Judd Baker
Proverbs 3: 5-6

Chas. L. Judd

Rural Missouri House Calls

The Life and Adventures of Dr. Charles L. Judd

Serece Judd Baker

authorHOUSE®

AuthorHouse™
1663 Liberty Drive
Bloomington, IN 47403
www.authorhouse.com
Phone: 1-800-839-8640

First published by AuthorHouse 5/18/2009

ISBN: 978-1-4389-5745-6 (sc)

Library of Congress Control Number: 2009903604

Printed in the United States of America
Bloomington, Indiana

This book is printed on acid-free paper.

Preface

Kirksville College of Osteopathic
Medicine 1940

Unionville - 1988

This book is about my father, Dr. Charles L. Judd. He was a friend to many, and a caring physician to all who called upon him.

The people you will meet in this book are his patients, friends and family. Some of these people are unusual; some are colorful and interesting in their own right. Some came as patients with very serious conditions. Most of the patients came to this family doctor with broken bones, poison ivy, pregnancy, tonsillitis, appendicitis and many other ailments common in small towns and rural areas.

Dad lived all of his life in the geographical middle of the country. He was born near Newtown, MO in Sullivan County, and went to college in Kirksville, MO in Adair County. He practiced medicine first in Pollock, MO in Sullivan County and then in Unionville, MO in Putnam County. He doctored many people in these three counties for 64 years from 1940 until 2004 just three months before his death.

In the 1940's in rural middle America there were no TV's, microwaves, MRI's, CAT scans, Mammography, Sonograms, electron microscopes, latex gloves, or even antibiotics, except for penicillin. There were no pills to go to sleep, no pills to wake up, no pills to lower cholesterol, nor even pills to keep you from getting pregnant. There was no chemotherapy for cancer, no transplants for diseased organs, nor by-pass surgery for clogged arteries.

This book represents the best of my recollections about my father, his patients, and their families. It also represents the written work of a number of people identified in the text and the memories of Dad (Dr. Judd) as told to me, and in some cases, recorded for me on cassette tapes. Most of the people have been identified by their true names because I want the world to know what great people I had surrounding me as I grew up.

Introduction

It has been a privilege to grow up in the loving community of Unionville, Missouri where my father was the beloved doctor to many people for over 60 years. Dr. Charles L Judd belonged to the whole community, including all of Putnam and Sullivan County, and I learned very early in life that he belonged to all. My mother and I always had to share him. There were very few times I can recall spending time alone with him until the last few years when we had many days of sharing the events of the 1900's.

This book is an attempt to explain the life and times of Dr. Charles L. Judd and the communities and people that were so dear to him. I have spent the past 10 to 15 years gathering material to include in these pages and the dilemma has been 'where do I start'? The 87 years that my father was on this earth brought hard times, easy times, fun times, and sad times. I will attempt to tell these stories as truthfully and clearly as possible.

As anyone could imagine, I would never have accomplished this writing alone. First I want to thank my **Heavenly Father** who has given me faith and trust in the people of my life, as well as the security in my future home with Him in Heaven.

Next, I want to thank my **Earthly Father**. Without him there would be no story. He spent many hours. as we drove around the countryside, recording the events of his life on tape for me. I thank him for living the kind of life that is worth the telling. I'm not naïve enough to think he was perfect or always right for I recognize that he was a human and, as such, made mistakes during his life. But I must say, I believe he had a pure heart and wanted to please and do what was right and good for his patients and friends.

A big thank you goes to my husband, **Ron Baker**, who is an inspiration as he kindly allows me to pursue all my projects and run down different rabbit trails everyday. He spends hours proofing my efforts, keeping our family of five adult children and six grandchildren running smoothly and serving our fellow Christians in our church family. He even finds time to complete lots of 'honey do' jobs for my 90-year-old mother who lives near us.

My mother, **Ruth Judd**, has lived near my family for 33 years, and she's been a strong, healthy influence for us all. She has spent many hours taking care of kids and grandkids over the years. She's a wonderful cook and always ready and willing to help us all. She still lives in her own home, drives anywhere in Lee's Summit she wants to go, and takes care of all her personal needs. She was born into a family with nine children and survived the depression years of the 1930's. I guess she thought that having only one child would make life simpler; however, I wanted a big family and so she got into care giving in a big way again.

Another thank you goes to **Duane and Kay Crawford** whose books have encouraged me to proceed with this one. Some of the articles and ideas in this book are strictly theirs, and I have been given permission to include them.

The pencil sketches in the book were created by **Ron Raymer** for the first booklet I put together for Dad in 1990. Thank you Ron for this contribution.

I want to thank my dear friend **Kandi Lorenz**, who took time out from her very busy schedule as Executive Secretary for Pastor Fred Allen at Lee's Summit Baptist Temple, and all the other varied tasks she performs weekly. She did the final edit for me, dotting all the i's and crossing all the t's.

Other contributors to whom I am indebted include but are not limited to, **Nina Rexroat, Glenda Mills, Gloria Rhoads and Janice Doolin,** (nurses), **Melvin Hall, Bill Schnelle,** and the many patients and friends you will read about in these pages. A valuable resource was also the wife Dad had the last seven years of his life, **Carolyn Smart Bomgardner Judd**. In those years she cooked for him, kept house and office for him, listened to his many stories and made it possible for him to stay in his beloved Unionville seeing patients everyday until the last few weeks of his life. Dad NEVER retired!

Unless otherwise noted, all the manuscript in this book is in my own words and is as factual as I know how to make it.

Serece (Judd) Baker

Calendar of Events

Dr. C.L. Judd – Medical Practice

May 23, 1940
Graduated – Kirksville College of Osteopathic Medicine

June 24, 1940
Officially Opened Practice – Pollock Missouri

September 8, 1940
Married Ruth Edmunds

January 1, 1944
Bought 1/2 interest in Monroe Hospital and Clinic

January 4, 1944
Father, William Harvey Judd dies

January 18, 1944
Daughter, Nola Serece, birth

January 1, 1945
Moved to Unionville

October   1948
Added new addition to Monroe Hospital: 10 rooms, elevator, operating room to meet new state laws regulating hospitals

November 2,   1962
Bond passed to build Putnam County Memorial Hospital (PCMH)

July 1   1963
Dr. G.G. Gray Joined Staff

October 13, 1963
Patients moved from Monroe Hospital to PCMH

April   1964
Ground Breaking for new Monroe Clinic
August 1967
Dr. Phillip Brackett Joined Staff

July 1   1980
Sold Clinic and Practice to Kirksville College of Osteopathic Medicine (KCOM)

May 1980
Celebrated 40 years in Practice with an open house at the Scout Building

June   1981
Dr. Stephen Casady begins practice in Unionville

June   1982
Dr. Mark O'Brien began practice in Unionville

July 1, 1984
Dr. C.L. Judd announced retirement

July 14, 1984
First Major Heart Attack for Dr. C.L. Judd

October 4 1984
Dr. Judd moved to Lee's Summit, MO with his daughter and her family

February 3, 1986
Dr. Judd moved back to Unionville

May 23, 1986
Bought Altes Building West of Square and resumed medical practice

December 6, 1988
Had quadruple by-pass surgery – St. Luke's Kansas City

July 15, 1990
Celebrates 50 years in medical practice at Schooney's - North Highway 5

Nov. 14, 1997
Married Carolyn Smart Bomgardner in Unionville

June 2004
Fell and broke three ribs and Dad and Carolyn stayed in Lee's Summit as he tried to recover

August 10, 2004
Dr. C.L. Judd died at the home of his daughter and son-in-law, Serece and Ron Baker in Lee's Summit, MO

Part I

The Last Two Years With Dad

2003 - 2004

Chapter 1
Dr. Judd at Work in 2003-2004

Hellooooo

Helloooo, pardon me I couldn't hear you!!!

That's how the phone was answered at the Judd residence, which also served as the medical office for Dr. Charles L. Judd in Unionville, Missouri, a small town about eight miles south of the Iowa line and just about midway across the state on Highway 136.

The voice on the phone didn't belong to a receptionist but to the doctor himself. At 87 years old he was the oldest practicing doctor in the state and maybe the country.

If you needed surgery or had a bad heart, he would send you to one of the younger doctors in town or to Kirksville, just 45 miles away. But if it was the flu, a sore throat, minor injury, poison ivy or bee stings, patients would take a seat in the living room and soon they'd hear "Who's next"? Much visiting went on in that living room.

He didn't take Medicare or insurance, but charged from $10 to $15 for a visit, depending on what services were required. The front door was unlocked and the patients just walked in and took a seat. Patients came from all over the area, including southern Iowa and the four counties in north Missouri of Putnam, Sullivan, Mercer and Adair. In the last few years he treated old order Amish and Mennonite families who had moved to the area. Carolyn said, "Doc's in there charging the people for his services and I will soon go out and collect free fertilizer". They would tie their horse and buggy up just outside the office. Besides the local folks a few families even came from as far away as Kansas City (a three hour drive) because Doc was the only doctor they had ever known and they knew he personally cared for them, and they trusted him. He delivered over 3,500 babies, and in some families that included three generations. He has treated five generations for several families. There were two families for which he delivered eleven children each.

Kathy Campbell had been seeing Doc Judd since she was very young and she said, "Everybody around here knows Doc and we don't know what we'll do if he every quits." He actually retired in 1984 and soon after had a major heart attack. For the next two years it was necessary to live in Lee's Summit, Missouri with my family, and me but he didn't really recover fully until he moved back to Unionville where he'd practiced medicine since the early 1940's.

After returning to Unionville, he tried to stay retired, but too many people still needed his services and he would rather be taking care of his patients than doing anything else on earth.

In 1986 he bought one end of the old Altes Feed Store, which had been converted into a cozy two bedroom apartment by Glen and Peggy Davis, just one block west of the town square and right on Main Street (136 highway).

Even twenty years later, it seemed there was always somebody in the living room waiting to see the Doc.

His wife of six years, the former **Carolyn Smart Bomgardner**, kept the home neat with fresh flowers in the living room on the coffee table beside a dish of candy with delicious smells coming from the kitchen as she prepared the noon meals. All summer and fall she was busy 'putting up' the produce that many patients brought to their home. You could find Doc first in line at the city park farmer's market to buy produce and baked goods. There were strawberries, green beans, corn, turnips, onions, tomatoes, zucchini and yellow squash, apples and blackberries. Early spring produced lettuce, spinach and radishes. He loved the baked goods and usually brought home a pie or fresh baked bread from **Mrs. Brown** or **Mrs. Jones**. **Bill Schnelle** kept him supplied with fruits and vegetables all season and so Doc affectionately nick named him 'Vegetable Bill'. Late in the fall **Mr. McDonald** would always leave a feed sack full of turnips. Doc loved them raw or cooked and could eat them every meal.

Taped on the kitchen cabinet was a Snellen Eye Chart for driver's physicals, for school kids athletic physicals and for the Department of Transportation physicals. Every fall Doc, along with the other doctors in town, **Dr. Casady**, **Dr. Abid**, and **Dr. Williams** would go to the school and give the physicals for all the athletes in Putnam County Schools for free. That was the job that he and **Dr. L.W. McDonald** had also done since the 1940's. If they happened to miss the free clinic they could get it done at the office later for just $5.

Most mornings were busy and it seems there was usually somebody waiting in the living room. There were many who couldn't afford to go anywhere else, but there were also many who had doctored with him their entire life. On an average day, at age 87, he would see 10 to 20 patients. During the slow times he would read the paper or watch sports on television.

Dad graduated from Kirksville College of Osteopathy in the spring of 1940 and moved to Pollock, Missouri to begin his lifelong career. Just because his practice seemed to be from a different era didn't mean he wasn't up on all the latest medical research. He would read journals and attend seminars and update classes several times a year.

There was a sample cabinet in the bedroom where Dad kept meds left by visiting drug representatives. One day in 2003 a teenager came by to get a prescription for some allergy medicine and Dad knew he couldn't afford much so he gave him some samples. The boy asked how much he owed and Dad's reply was, "Nothing, and don't try to bargain with me either."

He always had a story to tell and everyone from teenagers to his old buddies at the coffee shop, every morning at 8:00, enjoyed a good joke regularly. He never forgot a punch line.

His daily routine seldom varied. Up at 6:00 am and in the shower, after which he would eat a bowl of cereal with a banana cut into it (for potassium you know). Then it's off to Ryals' Service Station where the good ole boys gathered to wait for the Kansas City Star to be delivered as they drank coffee and shared tales. Carolyn called the daily gathering "The Liar's Club". About 8:30 he was off to the post office to pick up the mail and then home by 9:00 to put out the 'open' sign for the day. He never left the house without leaving a message on his answering machine to let people know where he had gone, how long he'd be gone, and when he would return home. He had a habit of leaving the garage door open so that people could see that he was home when they drove past. He didn't want to miss seeing any of his patients because he really liked visiting with each and every one of them. I guess you could say, "He was born to serve".

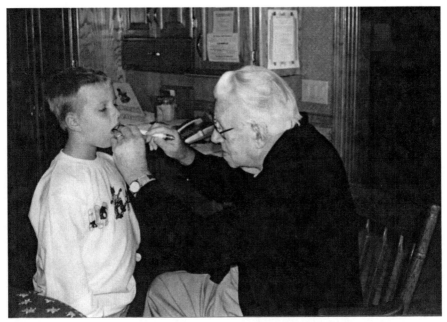

Great Grandson, Quinton Judd Lewis, is being examined for a sore throat.

Chapter 2
"So Long, Doc!"
By Duane Crawford

This tribute appeared in the Unionville Republican in August 2004

A distinguished citizen and leader, he was one of our community's main pillars. He was a devoted husband, father, doctor and friend who put community before himself. A legend to those of us who knew him best, his legacy did not rest with wealth, status or glory. His gifts to the countless people whose lives he touched came in the form of sacrifice, unselfishness, compassion, love, and a sense of humor.

We all mourn our old country doctor, but we will never forget the goodness of this remarkable man. Quiet, dignified, modest and gentle, he was larger than life to all of us. To the thousands from three generations who admired, respected and trusted him, he was always known as "Doc."

Doc's doctoring credentials go back to an age when Midwestern roads were mainly dirt, when house calls consumed a major part of a doctor's life and when medical technology consisted of little more than a doctor's skills, a tiny bag of instruments and some pills. It was a time when doctors rode horses or mules or bulldozed their Model A Fords through mud and snow to reach patients on some lonely country road. It was a time when a doctor's personal life took a backseat to his patients. Because he was so devoted to his patients, vacations for Doc were few and far between.

Few doctors could ever match Doc's record of medical achievements. Throughout the years of his medical practice, Doc delivered over 3,500 babies and a litter of pigs. He often joked, "I guess I did my part for the American labor force." In many local families, Doc delivered three generations of babies. He often said of those families, "Yeah, I delivered the father, the mother, the kids and the kids' kids."

As for the litter of pigs, Doc came to the aid of a local farmer who needed help with a precious sow. Because the local veterinarian was on a call and couldn't get there in time, Doc received a message from the desperate farmer. With the farmer and a neighbor serving as midwives, Doc surgically removed the babies and sewed up the sow. Mother and babies survived and made it to market.

Doc's business of delivering babies was not confined to Putnam County. When the Midgets played the Milan Wildcats in their annual football war, Doc had sufficient reasons to root for both teams. He had delivered all but one player from both teams and the Milan Coach, **Duane Schnelle.** That included 19 players and the coach.

Born on December 23, 1916, on a farm near Newtown, Missouri, during a blinding blizzard, he was the youngest of **William Harvey** and **Catherine (Reed) Judd**'s four sons. A daughter was born eight years later. Because **Doc Kimball** couldn't get through the storm that night, two midwives were tasked with the responsibility of helping with **Charles L. Judd**'s entry into the world.

Like most children of his time, Doc's education began in a humble one-room schoolhouse. Attendance at Newtown High School meant riding a horse six miles a day, but a doctor ordered that to stop after Doc came down with pneumonia during his sophomore year. He transferred to Powersville High School and graduated in 1935.

With thoughts of being a teacher, Doc attended Kirksville Teachers College in Kirksville, Missouri, but surgery for appendicitis derailed his plans. While recovering in the hospital with nothing to do except pester nurses, he wrote a humorous poem about his bedridden dilemma. That medical experience convinced him to practice medicine.

Following graduation from Kirksville College of Osteopathic Medicine in 1940, Doc bought a Model A Ford for $35, packed his meager belongings and headed to Pollock, Missouri, to begin his practice.

A fine lady named **Aunt Meg Wells** adopted him on the spot, and she provided room and board for $20 a month. A bank loaned him some money to rent an office behind the bank, a furniture dealer loaned him a few pieces of furniture on time, and a garage let him open a charge account. He was ready for business.

Doc has never forgotten that first house call. It came from a frantic husband whose wife was beginning labor. Grabbing his bag, he cranked up his Model A and made a beeline to the house. After the successful delivery, he was paid in cash, which was unusual during the Great Depression.

"My fees were usually paid in pigs, chickens and eggs," Doc has often said. "Folks didn't have money. After I'd make my round of house calls, my car looked like a produce truck heading for market." Doc never worried about a bill and he never sent one out. "Some took advantage of me," he admitted, "but most folks eventually paid in some way."

Bill Davis tells this story about how he and Doc became lifelong pals: "I drove a produce truck for **W.E. Ross** and Pollock was one of my stops. A tornado roared through town one day, and I dove for cover. Suddenly, out of nowhere, this little fellow with a black case came tearing down the hill to check for injured people. When I asked who that character was, someone answered, "Oh that's Doc Judd. He's our new town Doc."

Seeing a need to improve medical service in Unionville, Doc took out a loan and purchased part interest in the Monroe Clinic in 1944. From then on, he split his time between his Unionville and Pollock patients.

Before long, Doc joined forces with another extraordinary doctor by the name of **L.W. McDonald**. Together, the two provided Putnam County and surrounding counties with top quality care at affordable prices. The two were instrumental in making the Putnam County Memorial Hospital a reality in 1963.

Many male and female Midget athletes have fond memories of Doc Judd, because he was always there for them. For as long as coaches, players and fans can recall, Doc volunteered his time to give player physicals without charge. At athletic events, he was always nearby in case a player on either team needed medical attention. During an important football game one year, he received a call that he was needed to deliver a baby. He rushed to the house, delivered the baby and sped back to watch the game. Doc was an avid Midget supporter in every sport.

For over 50 years, Doc was Putnam County's coroner. Although he had many coroner cases through the years, the crash of the Continental Boeing 707 northwest of Unionville on May 22, 1962, was his biggest challenge. All 45 passengers and crew were killed.

As the coroner, Doc took charge. While in the national spotlight, Doc had to make tough decisions and had to work closely with the FBI, the airline and Missouri's attorney general. After the investigation ended and the mountain of tedious paperwork was completed, Doc received numerous letters of praise for the manner in which he conducted his duties.

Besides his unselfish giving of contributions to local causes through the years, Doc never forgot his profession. In 1975, he was designated a distinguished patron for donating $15,000 to the Kirksville College of Osteopathic Medicine. And in 1984, he gave $50,000 to the same institution.

Through the years, Doc has received many awards for his achievements. For his lifelong dedication, hard work and commitment to our community, the Missouri House of Representatives Resolution was passed and presented to him in 1996. Also, the same year, he received a Distinguished Service Award for Outstanding Contributions to Interscholastic Programs in Northeast Missouri. And there were other awards.

Doc had a renowned reputation for storytelling, and everyone's ears perked up when he said, "Did you ever hear the one about . . .?" He seldom told the same story twice.

Even after a series of medical setbacks in recent years, Doc continued to stay active in the community. He faithfully followed his beloved Midgets whenever his health allowed. Doc and his lifelong pals, **Aaron Stuckey, Bill Davis, Leonard Johnson** and Don **Herrick** would congregate at Ryals Convenience Store on most mornings to have coffee and reminisce.

On patriotic occasions he was always present. One year near Memorial Day he showed me a poem he wanted to recite for the occasion and asked, "Do you think it's too long?" The title of the poem was: "Just a Common Soldier." "If that's the one you want, recite it, " I answered. "The title fits you, because you consider yourself just a common doctor." He's been reciting that poem on every Memorial Day since that day.

Despite slowing down a bit, Doc continued his medical practice from his home. Patients from all over southern Iowa and northern Missouri, and as far away as Kansas City came to be treated. They needed him, and he cared about them. Doc didn't accept Medicare or insurance, and a visit with Doc usually cost no more than a few dollars. For a number of years, he was the oldest practicing doctor in Missouri.

His daughter, Serece, said a few days ago, "Dad simply wouldn't retire. While he was recovering at my home in Lee's Summit during the last month of his life, he was still seeing patients. He just couldn't turn people away."

On November 22, 1998, Doc proudly received his 60-year Masonic Service Award. He seldom missed a meeting. He was also a faithful member of the First Christian Church of Unionville, usually attending the early service.

When I visited **Marc Hounsom** at the Putnam County Care Center last Saturday, he described the true value of the giant of a man. "Doc, Marc said, "can not be replaced. About a month or so ago Doc came in to visit with me and stayed for almost an hour. He told a few stories, and we talked about yesterday and today. We will miss him."

And so, . . . we have lost a true champion of the common people. Our old country Doc has left us and entered the gates of Heaven. **"So long, Doc!"**

Duane Crawford, Journalist and friend

Part II

Dad's Childhood Days

1918 – 1939

Chapter 3
A Stormy Beginning

It was December 23, 1916 and a severe blizzard was beating against the little farmhouse about eight miles southeast of the small village of Newtown in the northern Missouri county of Sullivan. **William Harvey Judd** (3/11/1885 – 1/2/44) and his wife **Catherine Isabelle (Reed) Judd** (7/22/1886 – 10/5/71) were about to become parents of their fourth child. They already had three sons, **James Edgar** (1/3/1906 – 8/22/1984), **Howard Thomas** (6/16/1908 – 3/5/1983) and **Claude Rammel** (5/14/1912 – 12/23/1996)

This snowy night, **Dr. Kimball**, could not fight the raging blizzard to make the eight mile, dirt road trip to the Judd farm. But that didn't stop **Charles Lenny** (12/23/1916) from being born that night. Maternal Grandmother **Flora Taylor** and a neighbor "Aunt" **Lucindy Pigg** helped with the delivery of the ten pound baby boy. A few days later Dr. Kimball made it to the farm, circumcision tools and birth certificate blank in hand. It was eight years later that a sister, **Ruth Helen** (7/29/1924 – 2/10/2003), was born.

Charles, age 7 months, summer 1917

Two years after Charles was born, his father purchased the "**Jerry Tucker** Farm" and the family packed and moved two miles north on Route K.

William Harvey (Harv) Judd was a farmer and a veterinarian, and he was very busy with his practice in the years his young family was growing up. The depression hit everyone and times were tough and often he treated sick animals for no pay at all. He had one brother, **Edgar Judd**, who lived on a farm just a mile or so down the road. Edgar and his wife Ella had one daughter, Mildred. Harv's wife, **Catherine Isabelle (Isa) Reed Judd**, wasn't a stranger to work in those days either. She had five children, and with their help she planted a garden every spring. From the produce of the garden she canned vegetables (green beans, tomatoes, carrots, peas, etc.), fruits (peaches, apples, strawberries, etc.) and she even canned meat for the family. Isa walked with a slight limp and had one short arm from the polio she had as a young child. Her father, **Thomas Reed**, died when she was 11 months old and later her mother **Flora** married **James E. Taylor**

and they had four more children; **Jacob Ray Taylor**, **Wineva Taylor Collins**, **Flo Taylor Bowers** and **Charles Basil Taylor**.

Father William Harvey Judd Age 16

Mother Catherine Isabelle Reed Age 15

Chapter 4

Education and Schools

In the 1920's the country sides of rural Missouri were dotted with one room school houses, and the older Judd children attended Center Point School until they moved to the Tucker Farm. They then went to Center Grove School about six miles east of Newtown, Missouri and 1 1/2 miles from the farm in Sullivan County.

There were usually less than a dozen children in attendance and for the school year of 1926-27 Miss **Blanche Summers** was the County Superintendent, followed by Miss **Hildred Spencer** in 1927-28. Miss **Jessie Johns** was the classroom teacher during that time. She was a graduate of Princeton, Missouri High School and then a student at Maryville State Teacher's College. In the early days of education our country teachers didn't have to have a college degree to get employment, and sometimes they were only a year or so older than their oldest students. Grades 1 through 8 were all in the same room with the same teacher preparing all the lessons. In the center of the classroom stood a coal burning stove. The teacher or some of the students had to get the fire going in order to warm the schoolroom on cold winter days. The children not only studied the traditional reading, writing and arithmetic, but they performed in school plays, organized clubs (4-H and Health Club) and memorized many poems and spelling words. Dad received an award for having a perfect spelling record for all 12 years of school. He never missed a spelling word in all those years. Later it was determined that he had close to a photographic memory and had no trouble memorizing long poems, spelling words and school lessons.

Some of the teachers at Center Grove included **Mary Brantley** (later the wife of Jim Judd) and **Jim Judd** (Charles' oldest brother). Mary was a graduate of Newtown High School and Northeast State Teacher's College (called the Normal State College and now Truman State University) and taught at Center Grove when Charles was in the third grade. By the time he was in the sixth grade his brother, Jim, was his teacher. In 1931 Mary Brantley married Charles' oldest brother, Jim and they spent the remainder of their work years in administration and teaching in several schools throughout Missouri, including Powersville, LaGrange, Mexico, Spickard, Green City, Unionville and St. Louis.

When Charles was in 4th grade the children put together an Annual called the 'Blue and White'. From this book one can see the students that year included **Claude Judd, Mary Lou Tucker, Madeline Geosling, Forest Howard, Grace Howard, Zelta Cooley, J.D. Barnett, Zella Cooley, Charles Judd and C. W. Tucker.** In the 1927-28 school year two new first graders were added to the roll and those two young ladies were **Dorothy Jean Tucker and Mildred Judd** (Charles' cousin).

After grade school, the Judd boys went to high school in Newtown, over six miles northwest of the farm. They had to ride horses to go to school, so their dad built a little barn over at their Grandma Taylor's house in Newtown to keep the horses. The barn had room for two horses, and the boys would haul hay and grain over there in the fall. When they got to town in the morning they would put the horses in the barn. They would then go during the noon hour to water and feed the horses. They would eat the lunch they had taken since there was no such thing as a lunch program. When it was bitter cold their sandwiches would freeze. They thought it was a miserable ride to school, especially since they had gotten up early to do chores. They would get home late and have to do chores again. This was true for most of the students so they did not have much entertainment at school. Usually there was a Halloween party, Christmas party and maybe a picnic at Easter. That was the total of all the activities. They did play basketball in the fall but they had to quit early because of the weather. They played outdoors on a dirt court and it would get too cold to play late in the fall. They would also play a little baseball in the spring. The first year Dad was in high school the school didn't have electric lights, but they put them in his second year. They didn't have any restrooms in the school, and as Dad always said, "We didn't have a bath, we had a path". It got mighty, mighty cold to go out there, but they were used to it.

Every now and then they'd get into a little trouble. One time they almost got into serious trouble. A bunch of boys saw an old hand car on the side of the railroad track that the section foreman used to haul his crew up and down the track to work on the rails. These cars were operated by hand, sort of like a rowboat, and they would push a handle back and forth. One night the boys started down the track in that thing. They got it on the track because at the depot there was a thing that could lift it on, but it was very heavy and they couldn't get it off. They were a mile or so south of the depot when they heard a train coming. They got off and worked and worked, but couldn't get that handcar off the track. All they knew to do was to run, which they did. They ran back into the brush and that big old steam engine came through and literally tore the handcar into a thousand pieces. Parts flew everywhere. The railroad detectives were around for a long time trying to find out who did such a thing. Talk about a bunch of kids that kept something to themselves, they did! It was a long time before anyone knew what really happened.

In his second year of high school Dad developed pneumonia, which almost proved to be fatal. The doctor recommended that he not ride the six and one half miles on horseback in the future. By this time Jim and Mary Judd were in Powersville, Missouri (Jim was Superintendent and Mary teaching English). They invited Dad to live with them and finish high school. He did and graduated in 1935. He was always grateful to them for the opportunity they gave him to attend and complete high school. It was probably because of Jim and Mary's support and encouragement that Charles decided to go on to college and eventually become a physician.

This was the graduating class of Powersville High School in 1935. Dad is on the top row at the far right and his brother, Jim (top center) was the superintendent, math teacher and basketball coach.

From Powersville Dad went to Kirksville, Missouri to attend Northeast Missouri State Teacher's College to become a teacher or a veterinarian like his father. While in college, he became ill with appendicitis, and following surgery he was in the hospital for ten days. It was during this time in Laughlin Hospital that he made the decision to become an Osteopathic Physician, because he was so impressed with the work that the doctors around him were doing.

He went on to become a successful doctor, but had other talents as well. One was his ability to write poetry. The following poem was inspired by his hospital stay and has been published in several magazines.

Panning the Bed Pan
While recovering from an illness
I was terribly annoyed.
The toilet was denied me

And a bedpan was employed.
What I said about that bedpan
Could have landed me in jail.
And the agonies that I suffered
Prompted me to write this tale.

T'was in the early hours of morning
Just before the break of day
Came a warning so insistent
That I dared not disobey.
I was placed upon the bedpan
And it cannot be denied
Cold chills began to seize me
When the vessel touched by hide.
I was tipped back on my shoulders
And my legs grew stiff and numb.
The odds were all in my favor
That I'd die before I'd come.
In this upside down position
The leverage wasn't there
And with a mighty effort
I expelled a little air.

But when at last I got results
Then I grew sick with dread
I wasn't sure I'd hit the pan
Or piled it up in bed.
My heart was feebly fluttering
As I slowly raised my gown.
And there upon my spotless sheet
Was a hideous blot of brown.
But my troubles were not over
As I was soon to find
Because how could I maneuver
To wipe the place behind?
The muscles in my neck bulged out

As I stood upon my head.
I made a few wild passes
Then fell weakly on the bed.
It seems to me what would suffice
Is neither pan nor diaper
But a back adjusting thunder mug
With an automatic wiper.

Upon surviving this hospital stay (he was a much better doctor than a patient) Dad completed 60 hours of pre-med courses and began classes at Kirksville College of Osteopathic Medicine.

Before graduating from KCOM he found work in various places to supplement and support what his parents could offer him for his college years. The depression had hit everyone hard. Harvey Judd was a veterinarian, but he had five children, and a farm to manage, and it was very difficult to collect fees from the farmers, so money was scarce. Dad waited tables for his meals at the White Castle Café. One summer he even bummed a freight train to South Dakota and worked in the harvest fields.

While attending KCOM, although being a serious student, Dad also got into a little mischief once in a while.

The following stories are in Dad's own words:

"My Sophomore year in KCOM College we took dissection and we dissected a complete human body from head to toe. One of our buddies had a Model T Ford without a top on it and so one Saturday we went down to the section laboratory and fished out a body from the vat and put it in the back of the Model T Ford. One of us sat on either side of the cadaver and rode around the square in Kirksville. The police really didn't appreciate that but we talked them out of arresting us.

There was a Jewish fellow in school with us and he always wanted to pull some kind of a deal. There was a fellow by the name of **Owensby** who had a watermelon patch out at the southwest edge of Kirksville. We'd been going out there and buying watermelons for 10 to 15 cents each. He was a good ole boy and this Jewish fellow decided he wanted to steal the melons and we didn't want any part of that. He said that we just had to go with him and steal some so we went out to see Mr. Owensby and told him that we would be out this particular night and there was a fellow we wanted to play a joke on. We told him that when we got out by his watermelon patch for him to rise up and yell and start shooting and we'd scare this one particular student. We got in the patch and about the time we got situated Mr. Owensby rose up and said, "What the hell is going on here!" He started shooting that shotgun in the air and every time he'd shoot one of us would fall and yell and fall. We kept doing that every time he'd shoot and this fellow took off in a dead run down through the watermelon patch and the joke sort of backfired because there was a cultivator down at the end of the patch and he ran right under one of the shovels and cut the top of his head wide open. It knocked him out cold. We went down and got him and took him to the old ASO hospital and they worked him over and he came out of it. The first thing he wanted to know when he came to was, "How many of 'em died?"

Another incident happened, when I was a sophomore, and I was in the dissection lab. We had a late spring snow that year and this lab was in a half basement, the windows just about level with the outside ground. The instructor had to go to Jefferson City for something and there were over a hundred (maybe 150 or more) students dissecting these bodies. Of course because it was late in the spring we were almost finished with our dissection and the bodies were into pieces by then. With no instructor there to supervise we got a snowball fight going by reaching out the window and getting a handful of wet snow. Then it wound up that some students started throwing fingers, toes and pieces of liver and kidney or whatever was handy. They would have expelled us if they could of but they would have had to expel the whole class and they wouldn't even have a sophomore class. They did make us clean it up the next day and it sure wasn't the smartest thing we ever did.

My roommate, **Calvin Shad** and I lived in a house with quite a bunch of fellow students. Someone put itch powder in our beds one night and it nearly drove us crazy. We were pretty sure we knew who had done this so we decided we were going to get even with him somehow. When it got time to go home for Christmas (he had a Model A Ford) we took Limburger cheese on a stick and shoved it up in the manifold heater, which blew heat back into the car. We raked it off the stick and it melted up in there and this guy didn't get 10 miles down the road until he couldn't even breathe. I think we got even with him all right."

Chapter 5
My Childhood Days in Rural North Missouri
By Charles L. Judd

The following section includes the words of Dr. C.L. Judd as he recalls the many people who had an influence on his life in rural north Missouri. He dictated these words at the age of 84 in the year 2000.

"I started to school at age five. I think the folks started me because they didn't know what else to do with me since my older brothers all went to school and I wanted to go also. It was a mile and a half to walk or sometimes we'd ride the little Shetland pony and it didn't seem far then but it sure would now. We'd dress in heavy clothes and all through school we milked and took care of the sheep and hogs before and after school. We also helped mother around the kitchen with some chores because we didn't have running water and we'd carry water for her, especially on washdays. I remember one winter in the late '20's when it was not above zero for thirty days and that was real cold. When it did get up to 10, 15, or 20 above zero we thought it was summertime. The roads were drifted full of snow all winter long and of course back then there were no bull dozers or plows. The drifts were real high and we'd use sleds and horses for transportation. It was cold and the snow would freeze solid enough we could drive a team right over the fence and over the top of a fence and road and it wouldn't fall in or anything.

Back in those cold winters, we'd put up ice every year. We didn't have electricity for a refrigerator, so we had a regular icehouse and we'd put up ice off of the pond when it got cold. We'd pack it in saw dust and we had an ice box to keep milk and food in and everyday we'd have to bring in a chunk of ice to put in the box. We thought that was real nice when we could even do that. Now days people wouldn't want to do that. We could make ice cream in the summer with the ice we had saved. Usually the ice would last until September and then we'd have to use the cellar to keep milk and so forth. Each fall, Dad would butcher seven hogs and two fat steers because there were seven of us and he wanted a hog apiece and we also would eat the beef. We'd cure the pork (smoke it and cold pack it). Mother would cold pack the beef in half-gallon jars. If she only did it in quart jars you'd get a fight started because there were so many of us. Mother canned everything she could get hold of including strawberries, cherries, blackberries, gooseberries, applesauce, apple sausage, beef, beans, etc. and each morning after we had the chores done and before we started to school Mom would make biscuits. Every morning she'd have biscuits and gravy, steak or bacon and eggs, and hot cereal before we took off for school. Mother would make cornbread every noon and we'd have cornbread and milk for supper, along with things that were left over from dinner. To this day I still like cornbread and milk for supper. Dad always bought 15 to 20 bushels of apples each fall and we would store them along with potatoes, carrots, turnips, etc. in the fruit cellar.

Like most boys, we thought we had to smoke something when we were kids. So we would smoke grapevine or corn silks, whatever we could find. We had two or three large dogs and Dad had built a good-sized doghouse and we would go in there to smoke. One day Dad saw smoke coming out of the doghouse door and got suspicious and so he took a bucket of water and threw it in the door of the doghouse and nearly drowned us. We came running out of there and he said, "Oh, I didn't know you boys were in there, I thought the doghouse was on fire!"

About every Sunday in the summer we'd have either corncob fights or rodeos or something like that. At that time you could scare up 8 to 10 boys pretty quick in the neighborhood on Sunday afternoon. There wasn't anything else for us to do and we couldn't afford to go any place and we didn't have a car. I remember one particular Sunday afternoon; we were riding the steers, because we had a corral. We'd run them in the corral and into the shoot. Then we'd put a rope on them and let them out of the shoot. They'd come out buckin'. They'd throw us pretty high but sometimes it would be muddy and the ground and corral was not very solid. This day we got a steer that was wild and a little larger than the most of them. It was the neighbor boy's turn to get on one of them and he said, "I don't believe I want on that one." His father was there too, watching the rodeo, and he said, "Aw son, get on that steer, it won't hurt you. When I was your age I'd ride him." The son said, "When I get your age I'll say the same thing".

We used to have corncob fights and mud ball fights. We'd take a stick and make a mud ball to put on the end of it. We'd jerk the stick and it would come off and boy they did hurt when they hit you. The wet corncobs around the barn lot didn't feel very good either. We'd chose up sides and make forts. We'd do anything to entertain ourselves. We always found something to do.

I remember one thing I did one time that really got my rear end tanned. Dad brought some Limburger cheese home and oh does that stuff smell horrible as you well know. And when you put it on the stove it would just choke you and run you out of the house. I wasn't old enough to realize what it would do but my older brother told me to put it on the stove at school. I didn't know it would be so bad and we couldn't even stay in the schoolhouse. No one would own up to putting the cheese on the stove so one little girl, who saw me do it, told the teacher and I sure didn't like her after that because that got me a hard tanning; I really got whipped.

We had one teacher that was just out of high school himself and there were 15 to 20 good-sized boys going to school at that time, and he wasn't much older than some of the older boys. He couldn't control us at all. We wouldn't mind him at all or do anything he said. One warm February day we were having so much fun out on the playground and when he rang the bell at one o'clock for us to come in, we wouldn't do it. He came out there and was storming around trying to get us to come in and a couple of boys took the swing rope down and we backed him up to a tree and just tied him to the tree and wrapped the rope around him and the tree. We left him tied up for at least an hour (maybe more) while we played and then we turned him loose. When we turned him loose he went just across from the school grounds to **Matt Tucker's** (President of the School Board) and he resigned from teaching and said he had had all he could take of that bunch. They hired a lady to finish the term and she taught two or three years after that. She was a large, tall and muscular lady and when she walked in the schoolroom the first day (we hadn't had school for awhile) she had an armload of switches and paddles and she said, "Now I've been hired to teach at this school, and to have law and order and the directors have given me the right to do it. We're going to have law and order." There was a boy that had to try his luck and he threw an eraser at someone and she saw him. She brought him up to the front of the room and put him across the desk and gave him 15 licks with the paddle and I mean they were hefty ones and you know, to my knowledge she didn't have to work on anyone else the rest of the term. She had them convinced early and she didn't take any foolishness from anyone. Everyone respected her from then on.

When I was a youngster, I liked to hunt with my dog. This one particular hunt we got about a mile and a half along the road and my dog treed and I couldn't get her to leave where this hole was under a stump. So I started chopping and digging and finally got down to it and there was six skunks in that den and I killed all the skunks and boy did I smell. And my dog smelled and I tell you my mother wasn't very proud of me. She didn't think she'd ever get that smell off of me. But I managed to drag the skunks to the house and kind of made a thing out of a couple of sticks or poles I chopped down and I put them on that and got them to the house. I didn't know how to skin them but I wanted to because they brought a little money, even back during the depression. So I called **Jess Michael** of Michael's Foundation Company, and asked him if he would like to help me skin them for half and he said he would and he'd be glad for it, so he came over and we skinned skunks up into the night but it made us $18 apiece and that was a lot of dollars back in those days. I did quite a little of that and even caught a few mink which brought around $30 or more. Possum were only worth about 50 cents and we killed a lot of rabbits and we could get a nickel for them and rifle shells didn't cost but about 1/4 cent or maybe less so you could make a little money killing rabbits.

Each summer Dad and Uncle Ed would hire a girl to help with the cooking because mother wasn't too strong and we had a hired man who stayed with us (he didn't have both oars in the water all the time) who was a little bit dense about a lot of things. I don't think he'd ever had a girlfriend and when our summer girl came to work he just absolutely went crazy over her. He was trying to get her to go out with him and everything else and she didn't want to have any part of him. We'd go swimming in a deep pond by the house about every evening. Everyone had old- fashioned bathing suits and we'd have a barrel of fun diving off the old diving board. I'd been out in the pond swimming and I'd come to the bank to rest a minute where my Uncle Ed, who was quite a prankster, was lying on the bank. The hired girl started to swim across the pond and the hired man (who was crazy about her) took off right after her. He was swimming alongside of her and my Uncle said, "Dive off the board and see if you can swim under water and pinch her". I took him at his word and I gave a big leap off the board and I couldn't have hit it more perfect if I'd had radar. I was swimming under water and I swam up and grabbed her by the cheek of her behind and then I backed off and came up about 15 feet away from them. Boy, she was beating him over the head and calling him every name in the book. She said, "You, so and so, you pinched me!" and he said, "I did not, I didn't touch you!" To this she said, "You did too, you pinched me on the rear and I'm not going to have that!" She just kept a clobbering him and I almost drowned laughing and my uncle was just rolling over with laughter on the bank.

Insert picture 09 with caption: Charles and sister, Ruth, with farm dogs in 1927

Part III

The Pollock Years

Chapter 6
My Early Days in Pollock
By C.L. Judd

My days in Pollock were very important to me and I have very good memories from there. I rode horseback, in wagons, buggies, walked and I had a Model A Ford that I used in the mud. I sure went through a lot of mud in that Model A and sometimes it would get to rolling so I couldn't make it but I remember one occasion that **Murl Wilson** and **Clell Creason** helped me cut fences and shovel snow to get back from **Wyants** after their baby was born. My old red dog was faithful, staying right with me in the back end of the Model A and when I'd get stuck and get out, he'd get out. He'd get behind the wheel and the snow would just cover him up until he looked like a snowball.

Many of my Pollock friends have gone on; **the Anspaughs, the Camps, the Yardleys, the Wilsons, the Campbells, the Hollidays, the Wyants, the Herbert Rodgers**, all of those and their relations. And **Custer Rodgers, Schoonovers, Roseberrys, Leepers, Johns, McDonalds, Pearsons** and many, many more that I don't have space to mention. I cherish these memories and I still have a lot of friends there. They're descendents of the people that I just mentioned. They are the **Castos, Rodgers, Schoonovers, Camps, Cunninghams, Tuckers, Bushnells, Wyants, Johns** and many others. I also have a lot of patients and friends around the **Boynton** and **Milan**, areas. Also

Adair County in Missouri and **Appanoose** and **Wayne Counties in** Iowa.

My wife, **Ruth,** went with me on baby cases when we delivered them in the homes and she was very helpful to me. The day the big tornado hit we'd been out west of town on Sand Ridge delivering a baby and had just gotten home and gotten stuff put away and we had a full size rubber sheet (bed sized) and when the tornado hit it tore our house up quite a bit. It broke the windows out and it sucked that big sheet out the window and I didn't know where it went for several days. Finally, **Basil Sinclair,** whom I should have mentioned earlier, was carrying the mail and about 2 1/2 miles northeast of Pollock (he was on horseback) his horse kept shying around something in a ditch. Finally he got off the horse and looked in the ditch and there was my rubber sheet. He brought it back to town and gave it to me.

Around the town of Pollock there were many wonderful people as I've stated before and there were those that left quite an impression. **Punkin Holliday** liked the Spirits Fermenta quite well and he had a large family of which I delivered several. He was a distant cousin to **Jack Holliday** who had a grocery store in Pollock and he came in there one snowy night and he was just wet as a drowned rat because it was a wet snow and he was slightly intoxicated. Jack had a floor furnace and Punkin started taking off his clothes in front of the furnace. He took off his shoes and socks and shirt and Jack told him to stop because there were people in the store. Punk said, "By God, I won't and I'm a goin' to take them off". And he just kept a goin' and finally Jack yelled at someone by the door to open it and he grabbed Punkin by the nap of the neck and the seat of the pants and went over to the door and threw him out into the street with his wet clothes right after him. Jack said, "Now stay out there and don't you come back." I don't know where he went or to where he wondered off.

Another time there was a carnival in town or maybe an athletic show where they had wrestling and boxing. There was this great big old wrestler, a big rough guy, and Punkin had to carry rocks in his pocket to weigh 110 pounds but intoxicated as he was they offered him $5 to stay in the ring more than three minutes. Punkin decided that he'd make himself $5 and he got up on the platform and he pounded on his chest. He was so little and spindly he really looked funny up there with that big wrestler. They finally found some shorts for him to wear. They wrapped 'em around him two or three times and this big guy told him if he gets enough pound on the mat and he'd quit. So Punkin told him O.K. and they started the match. This wrestler got him up in the air and was twirling him around and around above his head with his hands and Punkin was a yellin' and a screamin' and finally he said, "Damn it, let me down to the mat where I can pound it. I can't pound the mat clear up here!" So the fellow just dropped him on the mat and boy he hit hard and he got up and went outside and leaned against a tree. He was really sick. He said, "That big #**#x#C##*** hurt me."

Another person I remember quite well was **Ready McCartney.** She worked at Jack Holliday's store for a long time and she was an Alexander. She was a wonderful lady. **Charlie Dearing** was another lady there that was a dear soul that everyone thought a lot of. Then there was **Mrs. Fanny Schoonover,** and oh so many more. **Chester Neighbors,** in the bank, was a wonderful person and was very accommodating to me and helped me in any way he could. **Creston Ollinger** was real nice and did a lot of things for me. **Rusty** and **Bertha McDonald** (Rusty had an arm off at the shoulder from a train accident) took care of our daughter, Serece, when she was little and they ran the crank and holler telephone system. If I was out on a call and someone else wanted me they'd call me at the place I was so I could keep going. Bertha made a wonderful secretary because she kept people informed as to where I was and how they could get a hold of me.

Lawrence Tucker was a magician and it was fun to have him entertain with his tricks. **Ray Board** was a mechanic and I always liked Ray and his wife **Beatrice**. They were real nice people. **Johnny Sears** ran the barbershop and I know one time there was a fellow that came into town and into Johnny's barber shop and no one knew him at that time (he eventually settled there). He'd begin telling about jobs he'd had over the years and how he'd worked so many years on this deal and so many years on that deal and so many years here and there. After he was gone I said (I was in the barber chair), "You know Johnny, I was just sitting here counting up on him and he's 120 years old right now if he's worked every place he claimed he has".

Herbert Rodgers was a real nice person too, and he was the barber after Johnny. I think he barbered in Boynton too. I always thought a lot of Herbert and his family and his son of course, who runs the grocery store in Pollock. **Virgil Rodgers** (Herbert's son) is such a nice individual and would accommodate anybody, anytime, anyplace. (More is written about Virgil and Bernice Rodgers and their Pollock store in Chapter 29.)

I remember a man in Pollock who had a goat with a little cart and harness with which he hooked him up. He led this goat to town to haul his groceries home for him. He tied the goat out in front of **Rhineharts's** store one day and went in to the store leaving the goat outside. While he was in there someone came along and poured High Life on the goat's back. That goat took off down the depot hill and by the time he reached the railroad track the cart was torn up and the harness was all torn off of the goat and he really scattered things up and down the hillside.

One night I had a call to this old ladies house in the country. Evidently her son, who was 50 to 60 years old, had tumbled over in the hog lot with a heart attack and when they found him the hogs had already started working on him a little. I was called down there to observe the body in the capacity of coroner and then it was six months after that that I had a call to see his mother. The roads were of course muddy so I took the jeep and **Hade Burns** went with me. We got down there and went into the house and the old lady was on a couch and the son she was living with said, "Ma, the doctor's here". She looked up and squinted one eye and says, "Ernie, is that the doctor that killed Franky?" I thought Hade Burns would never let me live that one down. He just laughed and laughed about that.

The babies were coming fast and furious back in 1940. One baby case was on Election Day. One baby was born east of town and I had another case going in town. I was running back and forth from one house to the other to see who was going to be first but we managed and got both of them here that day. I know **Bernard Camp** won't mind at all if I mention about him. That November in 1940 I delivered his first son and after it was over he wanted to know what he owed me and I told him I guessed $20. He said he only had $15 that he had saved up for Dr. Simpson (from Milan) who was on vacation at the time but was supposed to deliver the baby. I hold him that I'd do it for the same amount that Dr. Simpson said he would do it for and I took the $15 home and was very happy to get it.

That same year **Flossie** and **Pete Harrison**, and **John** and **Neva Lemon** had children born. **Evelyn Pearson's** son, **Jerry** was born that year too and this was my first six months in practice. It was very exciting to go to a country home and deliver a baby.

When I started practice we didn't have any antibiotics and if someone got pneumonia you nursed them through it with mustard plasters and analgesics and various things to control temperature. I gave them treatments and hoped that they pulled through. Luckily, most of them did recover well. We didn't have immunization shots like we do now and when we got an epidemic going, it was very hard to control. In fact we didn't have any way of controlling it at all. People would get measles, chickenpox, mumps, scarlet fever, whopping cough, diphtheria, polio and several other contagious diseases and all we could do was keep the fever down, rub ointment on to keep down the itching and quarantine them to keep others from being exposed.

I was a resident of Sullivan County because that was where I was born and raised and I hadn't moved my residence. Old Dr. Roberts was coroner when I went to Pollock and he was way up there in age and unable to do the job anymore. He was finishing out his term and I had already been elected to take office the first of the year. This was between the election and my taking over. Someone had committed suicide down by Reger, MO and it was quite a little way down there. Old Doc drove about 15 MPH and he had an old car called Old Bobby, a '27 Chevrolet Coup. He had the back end of that loaded down with samples when the prosecuting attorney from Milan called and said, "Doc, would you get Doc Roberts and come down to Reger? A fellow down there shot himself and old Doc drives so slow. A lot of times when we do call him, it will be the next day before he will come down. Will you go get him and get him down here so we can get this case over with before this body decomposes too much?" I said I'd try, so I went up to Doc's place to get him but he was very deaf. I told him what had happened and I offered to take him down to Reger because they want you as quick as you can come. He said that would be fine but Old Bobby won't run very fast. I had a V-8 Ford by that time and so we got on the way down the highway toward Milan on a rock rode. I was driving about 60-65 MPH, which was fast on a rock road. Doc chewed tobacco constantly and he had a great big chew in his mouth when he rolled down the window and spit out a mouth full of juice and it went out and came right back in his face and half of it on me and he wiped his face and rolled up the window and said, "How fast are we goin' son?" And my answer was, "Oh, I don't know". He said he didn't like to ride over 25 MPH and he thought we'd better slow it down. He didn't try spitting tobacco juice out anymore. Anyway, I took him on down and we got the deal settled.

Doc Roberts was the doctor in Pollock before I arrived and he was a great guy. One time Doc was up home in bed and it was a very cold night. A lady was sick out west of town and I'd been trying to get them to let me take her to the hospital because I thought she had appendicitis. She wouldn't go because she had always doctored with Old Doc Roberts and she wanted him to tell her she had to go to the hospital. I said I'd go up and get him and take him out there (about 7 or 8 miles from town to where they lived). I went up there and I liked to never got him awake, and his wife was in the other room and was ignoring me when I knocked at the door. She was a little different I must say and finally she came to the door and I told her I needed to see Doc about a consultation I thought had appendicitis. She said, "Well, he's in there in that north room in bed". There wasn't any heat in there and he had covers piled on him a mile high. I told him what I needed and he rolled the covers back. He was fully dressed and even had on his overshoes and overcoat and cap with earmuffs down and gloves on because that room was really cold. I got him up and we went out to see the lady. Sure enough he agreed with me that she had appendicitis and I took her to the hospital in Unionville and we did surgery on her that night.

One thing that happened back in the early forties when I was still living in Pollock and driving back and forth to the Monroe Hospital in Unionville had to do with a man named **Hi Over**. Hi lived in Mendota, which is about 10-12 miles northeast of Unionville. At that time there wasn't any hard surfaced roads out that way and the only road was 136 which was gravel (old #4 then running east and west) and highway 5 north and south, which was also gravel. There wasn't a thing toward Mendota that wasn't dirt and this fellow just kept getting sicker and sicker and they called and wanted to know if I could get out there. That was before my jeep and I knew that old Model A couldn't pull it. The mud was really rolling, so I said, "Well, I'll tell you how I can get there. The freight goes through here and I'll get on it. They'll let me ride the caboose I'm sure. I can come up on it and back on the passenger train that goes by about two hours later." So I got on the freight train and rode it up through Howland and on to Mendota. I walked over to Hi Over's house about a quarter mile away and he was desperately ill. I thought he had a ruptured appendix (which did prove to be true). We had to wait until the passenger train or doodlebug as they called it, came back from the north and we took Hi to the train with a team and wagon. He was awfully sick. Back to Unionville we took him down to the old Monroe Hospital and operated on him as soon as we possibly could. He did have a ruptured appendix but he survived it and I guess that shows that there's more than one way to get things done.

There was a fellow in Pollock by the name of **Jake Vance** and he always carried a bottle of High Life in his pocket. He never said much to anyone but just sat around on the benches in town. One day an Angora cat came by and was rubbing Jake on his leg. Jake got his little bottle of High Life out and poured it on the cat's back. There was a truck in front of **Jack Hollidays's** store and they had some boards for a runway out of the truck. The truck belonged to **Shrack's** from Kirksville and they were hauling groceries out of the truck and into the store on a wheelbarrow. When the cat took off he ran right up into the truck with the fellow pushing the wheelbarrow. The man ran out of the truck in high gear and yelled, "That cat has hydrophobia!" The cat then came tearing out of the truck, made two or three trips up and down a telephone pole and headed for home before the High Life cooled down. His master came out and wondered what in the world was going on with his cat.

One neighbor I had in Pollock would always watch every time I took off in the car and when I'd get home he'd be leaning over the fence between the two houses and ask, "Where you been Doc? Who was sick? What was wrong with them? What did you do for them?" He repeatedly did this, so one morning rather early, I guess I was a little tired, and I knew what was going to happen and maybe I lost my patience a little and I thought I'd cut him off at the pass. When I pulled in and killed the old Ford, he was waiting. He asked, "Where you been Doc? Who was sick? What was wrong with him?" And I said, "Well, he drank kerosene". To this he asked, "What did you do for him, Doc?" and I said, "I put a wick up his rear end and burned it out."

Newtown used to have a street fair every year and it usually always rained and got real muddy. This was a big event in our lives at that time and to me it was almost like the world's fair. It and the fair at Green City, when I was small were the high light of the year. There was a fellow by the name of **Albert Rash** that made taffy candy and sold it two pieces for a nickel. He had a big hook that he pulled it over and stretched it out and I thought that was the best stuff I ever saw in all my life. Speaking of the Rash family, there were twins by the name of **Ivory** and **Abe Rash** and one time a Unionville man by the name of **Charlie Cullor**, came over to give airplane rides (he had an old World War I Jeannie). He still has descendents around Unionville. He charged $1 a ride and Ivory and Abe went up with him and they were coming in for a landing and the plane clonked and sailed along for a little ways and then finally nosed down for about the last 50 feet from the wreckage and they were still hanging on to the seat. Luckily they weren't hurt but they were two scared boys. They took for town and that was all we saw of them.

While I was in Pollock **Ray Board** had a garage and **Frank Livingston** and **Jim Roseberry** also had a garage in town. It took them all to keep my cars running in all the mud.

I was coroner in Sullivan County from 1940 until 1944 because Doc Roberts didn't want to run for another term, as he was 80 years old. Then when we moved to Unionville I was coroner there for over 40 years. I served almost 10 four-year terms.

I had one coroner's case that turned out that it wasn't mine. East of Green Castle they found someone dead and thought it was in Sullivan County and so they called me to come down and I got there and told them I wasn't sure we were in Sullivan County. They were sure it was but we got a hold of someone that did know right where the county line went and we found out that it was in Adair County by about 15 to 20 yards. I had a long trip on those bad roads for nothing.

Chapter 7
Dr. Judd's Opening Speech
1973 Pollock, MO Centennial

Thank you, **Gene Wyant**, for the very nice welcome and I would like to re-welcome you all this morning. We should be thankful that this centennial had such a good committee and we should thank everyone in this community and in surrounding communities for the time, money, and tireless efforts that they put forth to make this possible. I think we should give everyone a big hand for what they have done for this community.

I didn't stay up all night preparing a speech because I speak seldom and slow and I think seldom and slow. It won't last long.

How many of you were here in 1873? Let's see the hands. How many of you expect to be here in 2073? Look at the optimist.

I am humbled and honored that the committee asked me to be the first on the program. Sometimes it is better to be first; sometimes it isn't. That makes me recall a story; and if you have heard it, close your ears. It's about the three gentlemen that were to be executed by the guillotine method. One of them was from France, one from Germany and the other was from a country next to Germany. I can't remember it; but if I could I would be afraid to say. Hitler overran it in 1939. When they got ready for the execution, the Frenchman was first; and the guillotine operator said, "Would you prefer being on your back or on your stomach when we put your head through the knife? " He said, "I prefer being on my back so that I can look up at the heavens." The guillotine operator pulled the rope. The knife fell about halfway and stuck. The guillotine operator let out an oath and said, "If they don't fix this, I'm going to quit. You can get up and go. If it doesn't behead you the first time you are a free man." So the Frenchman, very elated, jumped out of there and took off. The German came up next; and he said, "You have the same prerogative. Would you prefer to be on your back or on your stomach?" He said, "I also prefer to be on my back so I can look up at the heavens." The guillotine operator pulled the rope, and it fell about halfway and stopped for the second time. And he let out an oath and he said, "I am going to quit if they don't fix this. There's no use in even trying." He said, "OK, You're free; it didn't behead you." So the German got up and left. And the man from that country next to Germany came up and he says, "You, also, have the same prerogative. Which way do you want to be?" He said, "Until you get the damn thing fixed, I don't really want in there."

That makes me think of another story on a person of the same nationality that went down town one day. He locked his car and left. When he came back, he couldn't get the door open. He discovered he had left the keys in the ignition; so he called the police and wanted them to come down and open the door. And they said, "Where are you?" And he said, "I'm down at 19th and Plowed Ground Avenue, and please hurry." And so they answered, "We can't come right now but we'll be there later." And he said, "Well, I wish you would hurry; it's going to pour down rain and I left the top down.

Although I am not a native of Pollock, I am a native of this county and this community, as you well know. I came from Hell's Kitchen and there has always been something about Hell's Kitchen that I can't understand. You can't find it on the map, and everyone will lie to you about the boundary line. When I was a kid at home, the road ran north and south past the house. So a woman came by and said to my Dad, "Where is Hell's Kitchen?" And he said, "The road in front of our house is the west boundary. It's just across the road." But you could go a mile east to the neighbors on the north and south road and they would give the same story. You could start at Pollock and go west and they would say that the boundary line for Hell's Kitchen was just in front of their house. But if I am a native of Hell's Kitchen, I'm proud of it.

My first experience in this town was when I was approximately eight years old. As many of you older people will remember, my father was a veterinarian, and he went over the hills and hollows of this community taking care of the sick and afflicted livestock and I enjoyed going with him very much. This was a particular Saturday night that he had a call to see a cow with milk fever at **Myra** and **Manual Camp's** place. I know that many of you are related to them and their descendants – some of them are probably here. We arrived and Dad gave the cow a shot in the jugular vein and said in forty minutes she should be better but he would wait around to be sure. Dad gave me a dime and said, "Go up to **Chris Anspach's** Café and get yourself a bottle of pop and an ice cream cone." And a dime would do that in those days but it wouldn't even pay the tax on it today. So I hurried it up to town and it was a busy town on Saturday night in those days. I finally waded through the crowd and through the front door. The bar was full, and the restaurant was about half full but there was one stool at the counter and I hopped upon that stool. Chris said, "Whose little boy are you?" I told him I was Dr. Judd's son and he said, "I know him real well." I got my pop and ice cream and hadn't been in there long until I heard some loud talking. The language that was being used you usually don't hear in Sunday school. About that time the fists started flying and then it wasn't long until there was blood flying and my feet got itchy and I could hardly stay on that stool. I looked and there wasn't any way out of that front door; there just wasn't. Chris laughed at me and said; "Don't pay any attention to it, that happens all the time." Finally someone pulled a knife. I think it was an ordinary pocketknife but it looked like a bayonet to me when it came out of his pocket. Someone pulled a revolver. That was all my feet could stand. I jumped off the stool and I thought, "There's got to be a way out of here." I took right through the kitchen in a dead run with Chris right after me. I headed for the back porch and you old timers will remember that was a tall porch! Chris swore I took fifty steps in the air. I didn't go down the steps but just jumped off the porch. When I landed I was in high gear and I took for Manual Camp's place. When I got there I couldn't even tell them what was wrong because I was so out of breath. The first thing I said was, "Fight." Well, they knew what was going on and they laughed about it but Chris didn't let me live that down the whole time I lived in Pollock.

There was another fight after I came here to live and I won't mention any names. Two men were really battling and a little boy standing there kept yelling, "Daddy, Daddy," and I asked, "Who is your daddy son?' He said, "That's what they're fighting about.

I moved to Pollock after I graduated from medical school, May 18, 1940. I revved that late 1928 car I drove wide open down the big hill by the church, and hit the railroad track. The track was rough and the car was loose and it shimmied like a hula dancer but it held together and I made it up the next hill and pulled up in front of the old Farmer's Bank building. I switched the car off and it took it about three minutes to die because it was red-hot. That car was hell to start but it was also hell to stop after it got started.

The Bank Building also housed the Credit Union and I went to see **Chester Neighbors** who was operating the Credit Union at that time. I asked him if he thought there was room for another doctor in this town and he said he thought so. "Why don't you go talk to **Otis Reinhardt** and some of the business people around here and find out." He says, "Old **Doc Roberts** is getting old". Let me say here and now that Doc Roberts was a wonderful man. He gave much of his life going through mud, snow, hell and high water to care for the sick in this community. And I think at this time it would only be appropriate that we bow our heads in silent prayer in memory of Doc Roberts and all the people of this community that have gone on before us.

Bank Building in Pollock, Missouri where Dr. C.L. Judd had his first office in the back rooms from May 1940 until his move to Unionville and the Monroe Clinic in 1946

Thank you. Otis called Dr. Roberts and asked him if I could share the waiting room and use another room that was behind the bank building for an office and Doc seemed enthusiastic about it. Otis said, "We'll paper the rooms." I scrubbed the floors and stained around the ends where the congoleum didn't reach, bought some material for drapes and I see they are still there. I went over to **Reinhardt**'s and talked to **Ralph** and **Lela**, then on down to **Virgil** and **Meltha**'s and got a warm reception. Then I went across the street to **Jack and Mary Holliday**'s, stopped at **Johnny Sears**' Barber Shop and heard a few lies before going up to **Jim Roseberry's** Garage. Then it was on to **Melvin Casto's** Restaurant and then to **Verna Briggs and Henry's** Grocery Store. On across the street where the church is now stood **Everett Morlan**'s Drug Store. He was a good Pharmacist and had a good stock of medicines on hand. Then it was on down to see **Bertha and Rusty McDonald**. They were operating the 'crank and holler' telephone system. Next I went across the street to **Lawrence Tuckers** and down

44

to **Ray Boards**. Everyone seemed to be enthusiastic so I decided to move in.

As I was single I had to have a place to stay. Someone suggested **Aunt Meg Wells**. I don't remember who went with me but let me say here and now, she was the nicest lady I think I ever saw. She said, "Yes'm my son has gone to the army and I'm lonesome. I'd be happy if you would stay with me." She asked me the fabulous price of $20 a month for room and board. That doesn't seem possible to some of you that haven't lived through a depression. So I got my extra pair of shorts (I didn't have an extra undershirt) and a necktie along with a few other things and moved into Mrs. Wells' house. She had a bedroom for me with an outside entrance.

It was Sunday night and I was hoping for my first patient when my office opened on Monday morning. I was dreaming and anticipating the events of the next day when the phone rang two longs. I thought, "Oh, oh, they forgot the signal." But I thought I'd answer it and I did. They said, "Dr. Judd?" And that sounded a little odd and I answered "Yes, sir." He said, "Could you come out and deliver a baby?" It was eighteen miles southwest of town, out in the Judson neighborhood. I asked, "Who was supposed to do this?" I was new in town. But in those days sometimes no one was called until the lady went into labor. He said a doctor in Milan was supposed to deliver the baby but he was on vacation so would I come out and I said, "Yes, I'll be glad to." I think many of you remember that little square building out north of the bank building that had a little half moon and boards over the door; the one they turned over every Halloween night. I became so excited that it took three trips out there before I could leave town.

I finally got underway and went out there and it rained while I was there and I had a hard time getting home on the dirt roads. Also I was so excited that I had forgotten to tell Mrs. Wells that I was going to be gone. That poor old soul had worried all night about what had happened to me. I got home in time for breakfast and she fixed me a nice meal. I got paid $20 for that baby case which was the going price and I put it on the table and said, "Mrs. Wells, I'm going to eat and sleep for a month if I can't do anything else." And getting back to her once more, the hardest thing I have ever had to do was to go with the family to tell Mrs. Wells her son had been killed in action. We became even closer after that.

By September 1940 I married **Ruth Edmunds** and moved her to Pollock with me.

The March 15, 1943 tornado will be remembered by many of you. It was very destructive as it blew buildings away, turned some over and caused some to be burned up. It destroyed our house enough it was unlivable. Jack and Mary Holliday graciously invited us to stay with them. And after the excitement was over and people were patched up we all went to bed. In their spare bedroom they had a tall four-poster bed that one had to back off and run at to get into but we got in it. Just about the time we fell asleep the slats all fell out of the bed. We thought we had been hit by another tornado.

Many of you remember **Joe Mike Leeper**. I'll tell you what he said about the tornado. When it hit he thought it was going to do some damage where he was staying so he rolled up in a feather bed to keep from getting bruised up. In a few days he was in town and someone said, "Joe, what were you thinking about when you were rolled up in that feather bed?" "Well," he said, "I was thinking about all the mean things I had ever done and the storm was over. I just got up to fourteen years old."

Tornadoes do many strange things. The Holliday's 'john' and our 'john' sat back to back by the fence in the far corner of the yards. The storm reversed the toilets. They were picked up, tossed around, and were left upside down in the wrong yards. One lady had been tossed out of her house and got up with lots of splinters in her behind. Electricity was out and so I did the best I could to remove the splinters with a flashlight and tweezers.

Neighbor helped neighbor and everyone lived through the nightmare. The good people of Pollock helped one another and many life long friends were made while we lived there.

I want to tell a story on **Cooch Wilson**, whom many of you remember. We went fishing and hunting together and the first fall I was here Gooch didn't have a car and he said, "Doc, first day of the season, let's go hunting. I bought a bird dog, gave five dollars for him. Best dog in the country". I said, "Okay, we'll go." So when the season opened we loaded the dog in, got the guns, went out around **Sammy Olinger**'s ridge, got out of the car and started down through the field and that dog made the prettiest point you have ever witnessed. Cooch said, "See, what did I tell you. Look at that dog. Isn't that great?" About that time he broke point and jumped forward. Cooch said, "What in the ace is wrong with that dog?" I said, "I don't know anything about bird dogs." He did that three times and next thing we knew he nailed a skunk and a fight ensued. The air, you couldn't breathe it, the dog got sick and Cooch was going to kill him. I talked him out of it and after it got so he could breathe a little better I said, "Well, shall we go hunting?" He said, "Hell no, that dog couldn't smell a quail if he was roosting on the end of his nose." He put the dog on a long rope and we led him all the way back to town.

Before we left Pollock we were blessed with a daughter, Serece, who was two years old when we moved to Unionville.

C.L. Judd with daughter, Serece, on the porch of their first home in Unionville
which was a rental in 1946

I hold the people of this community near and dear to me and I have a warm spot in my heart because they gave me an enthusiastic reception when I came here and supported me well while I was here and I still have patients coming into my office that I took care of in the summer of 1940.

Chapter 8
Special Today!   Tonsillectomy

People were happy a new doctor had set up practice in their rural Missouri town. Several of the citizens got together and decided they wanted to have their tonsils removed. With liability the way it is today, no doctor would consider taking out six sets of tonsils in the office in one morning using only local anesthetic. But that didn't seem to concern young Doc Judd. Back in the 1940's people didn't sue much either and neither did they have any medical insurance.

Dad put these six people in a line, to take out their tonsils one by one, and after each surgery, he would drive them to their homes. The last patient was the local barber **John Sears**. John wanted his adenoids removed also. Dad said to John, "I don't think we'd better try taking your adenoids out in the office because I can't get to the area to numb it like I can the tonsils." To this John replied, "Oh, I'm tough, just go ahead and do'er Doc." With these instructions, Dad hooked into those adenoids with an adenitome up under the soft palate and clamped down. The perspiration popped out on John's forehead and ran down his face. Just as quickly as the adenitome was removed, John jumped up and headed out of the office on a dead run. He ended up in the middle of the street in front of the bank building. There he fainted, letting the blood run out of his mouth. Local citizens were walking all around and, of course, this scene made a good advertisement for the new young doctor in town. John was soon O.K. but maybe not quite so brave for the next procedure.

Chapter 9
Civil War Veterans

William A. Judd, Dad's great grandfather, was born on September 4, 1815 and died January 27, 1911. He was a circuit-riding preacher and was born in Kentucky. His parents moved to Kentucky from Pennsylvania before moving by covered wagon to Sullivan County, MO. Judd trained for the civil war in Sullivan County below the old Judd homestead as a Union soldier. He was 50 years old at the time the war started. He was captured at the battle of Shiloh and was held in Andersonville prison until the end of the war. He then returned to Sullivan County. His first wife died and he remarried at age 80. He remained married until his death at the age of 97 years. He and his first wife had 12 children, the youngest being **Joseph Judd**, the grandfather of **Charles Judd.** Joseph R. Judd born in June of 1855 married Margaret Denny and they had two sons, William Harvey Judd born March 11, 1885 and Edgar Franklin Judd born March 11, 1888.

William A. Judd, Co. B 53rd Regiment, Illinois was in the volunteer infantry. He enlisted in November of 1861. When the war was over he was granted $18 per month for the three months that he was in prison. Dad was privileged to treat three civil war veterans in his early practice in Sullivan County, MO. Matt Howell served with Dad's great grandfather, William A. Judd, in the 1860's and he was a patient until his death in 1942. **James Matthew Howell** was born in 1845. The other two veterans were **Marion Deeds** of Newtown, Missouri and

Niley B. Creason, who couldn't read or write but he hated **Franklin Roosevelt** with a passion and he wanted Dad to keep him alive until Roosevelt was out of office, but he died before that happened.

I still have the bass drum and the snare drum that was made by and played by William A. Judd in the Civil War.

Gravestones of Civil War veterans, William Judd (Dad's grandfather) and James Howell, one of three Civil War veterans Dad was privileged to have as patients until their death.

Chapter 10
The Sorghum Enema

Dad was called out to the country one day to attend to a lady who was unconscious. The trip to the farm home included riding a horse. At one point the horse had to swim across Locust Creek in order to get the doctor to his destination.

After arriving at the home, he determined that the lady was in insulin shock. Dad knew that he had to get some sugar into her system and do it fast.

Today, an intravenous (I.V.) drip with glucose would mean going in an ambulance to the hospital. Dad didn't have the choice to take the lady back to the hospital since it wasn't practical to swim back across Locust Creek.

The patient was in such a deep coma that she couldn't swallow anything, so the challenge was how to get the sugar into her blood system. Thinking fast, Dad asked her husband if he had any honey or sorghum in the house. When the man produced some sorghum, Dad put it in an enema bag with some warm water. He elevated the ladies hips and started a slow drip enema of the solution he had prepared. She soon recovered enough to begin taking sugar by mouth and made a complete recovery.

Chapter 11
Fishin' with Cooch

Cooch Wilson lived across the street from my parents, and his favorite pastime was fishing. He hollered from his front porch one day and said, "Let's go fishin' Doc." Dad's reply was, "Cooch, it's going to storm after while," (there were thunderheads and lightening in the northwest, and Dad always kept an eye on storms, especially after the tornado). To this Cooch retorted, "We're not made of sugar; we won't melt." Just the day before, Cooch had to stop mowing his lawn when it began to sprinkle because "it makes my arthritis act up." But when Cooch was goin' fishin' it didn't seem to make much difference what the weather was doing.

Cooch and Dad had a fish trap they made and submarined in Locust Creek (that was before the channel was straightened), and they were catching fish like mad. One morning they went out to empty the trap and they found the leaves had been disturbed that hid the chain, which held the trap. Someone had taken the trap, chain and all. Cooch did like to swear, and anyone who remembers him knows he could surely use the King's English to a disadvantage. This particular morning set off a storm of colorful expressions, but when Dad suggested they call the sheriff to investigate, Cooch exclaimed, "Call the sheriff? Hell, it's against the law to have a trap like ours." He had a habit of gritting his teeth and he said, "You know, Doc, a man that would steal a fish trap wouldn't be dead five minutes until he would be farther into hell than a pigeon could fly in three weeks." Cooch always had something like that to say about everything.

Chapter 12
My Parent's Early Years

During the winter of 1939, when Dad was a senior in medical school he met **Ruth Edmunds**. She was a beauty operator who grew up in eastern Illinois and then lived in Lamoni, Iowa. She had graduated from beauty school in Kirksville and owned her own shop in The National Bank building there. On September 7, 1940, the Reverend Hugh Harmon married them. The wedding took place at Grandpa Harvey and Grandma Isa Judd's home in Newtown. Uncle Jim and Aunt Mary Judd stood with them as witnesses. After a brief honeymoon to Bethany, Missouri and Lamoni, Iowa to visit her parents, **Mort** and **Lettie Edmunds**, they hurried home to Pollock so Dad could keep his practice going. Little did she know at that time that he had no intention of being very far away from his patients, ever.

In Pollock they took up room and board with **Mrs. Wells**. They lived there for about three months and then rented two front rooms from a **Mrs. Miller**, where they first set up their own housekeeping. During the four years or so that they lived in Pollock, they bought and lived in three different properties. One house they purchased for $500 and it was a right good house. They had running water put in from the well, and **Murl Wilson** remodeled the house and put in the water system. The last home they purchased there had been in the Reinhardt family. They stayed in that house until they moved to Unionville when I was two years old. The house is still standing and in pretty good shape thanks to the present owners, the **Waughs**.

Mom operated a beauty shop in their home during the day and traveled with my Dad on house calls at night or went with him to fill in at the hospital where needed. When I came along in 1944 that all stopped so Mom could take care of me.

The winter of January 1944, Dad's father had a stroke and passed away just two weeks before I was born. They named me Nola Serece. Nola was after Mom's oldest sister and Serece I think she just made up along with the help of a friend of hers. When people get over the sound and the spelling of the name Serece, they seem to like it, but it sure has been hard for me to educate people about how to say the name. You can only imagine how many ways it has been pronounced and spelled over the years; Cerise, Cherise, Serice, Shereece, Ceree, Sirece and on and on. Nola would have been easier, but some of the people started calling me Nodey and Mom didn't like that so when we moved to Unionville she started calling me Serece.

Ruth (Edmunds) Judd, Nola Serece and Dr. Charles L. Judd April 1944 – Pollock (Sullivan Country), Missouri

There were many sick people in the rural areas and bad weather made it hard to get to them. Once some folks came after Dad with a team and sled so he could administer to the sick in their family. This trip took all night in sub-zero weather. Another well remembered time was in the early spring when Mom and Dad went to the country to call on a patient (**Mrs. Lemons**), who had a bad heart. As they would say back then, the bottoms had gone out of the dirt roads from heavy spring rains. This trip also took all night. The Model A Ford chugged along, and by staying in the ruts made by wagons they were able to make the trip.

Many babies were delivered in the homes, and Mom helped when she could, going with Dad to assist in bringing new babies into the world. Many times these were all night tasks. Although there were some complicated cases, a breech birth, a cord around a neck and so forth, not one baby was lost. With God's help the missions were accomplished, and in the 50 years Dad was in full practice he delivered over 3,500 babies.

During the years Mom and Dad lived in Pollock, the country was at war. This made life more difficult than usual. Dad was called to serve in the war, but when he went for his physical, he was classified 4F. The army didn't want a man with a hernia, high blood pressure and bad teeth. He was disappointed that he couldn't serve his country overseas, but he tried to make up for it by serving those at home.

When we moved to Unionville in 1945 we rented a house next door to **Judge Casey and Dorothy Rose.** Later the folks bought a two-story house on West Main Street. Today that house has been torn down and the HyVee store stands in its place. We lived there for several years until I was in the 6th grade in 1956. That house had two apartments upstairs and we had roomers all the years that we were there. **Delsie McKinley** lived in one of the apartments. When she first lived there she was a telephone operator in town and later she worked for Mom at both the Flower Shop and the Dress Shop until she retired. **Lois and Ab Bonebright** lived in the other apartment for a number of years. When they moved out I had the run of a couple of rooms up there and I played there for hours on end with my paper dolls and Sears catalog cutouts of furniture and clothes. In 1956 we moved again. This time to a house south of town just outside the city limits. The home was built by the **Partin** family on their farm. Later **Dr. Robert McCalment** bought the farm, but the folks still owned the home there. That's where I lived until I left Unionville to go to college in 1962.

Enough with the houses we lived in and back to the days just at the end of World War II. Food was scarce in those days and everyone was issued food stamps for sugar, meat, and so forth. Mom and Dad had a garden and Mom canned many vegetables, fruits and even meat to use in the winter. Patients who butchered would pay them with meat, as well as with chickens and eggs Gas was rationed and care had to be taken not to use more than was necessary so the sick could be reached when needed. Mom was always a good cook and a hard worker. She helped her family and Dad's family many times with meals, and with clothing from the dress shop she owned and operated during the late 1950's and 1960's. During the 1950's and 1960's she also owned and operated a flower shop, which was really hard work. She bought that to help her brother, **Rollo Edmunds**, and his family of five children who had recently moved to Unionville from Hawaii. Rollo's wife, **Mary**, and Mom spent many all night sessions getting ready for weddings, funerals, proms and so forth.

My parents were married for thirty-three years and divorced in 1973. Dad married again that same year and in 1975 Mom sold the home in Unionville and moved to Lee's Summit, MO. Her greatest joy has been her five grandchildren (**Daniel** and **Matthew Lewis**, **Suzanne (Lewis) Stanley** and Ron's sons **Lance** and **Vaughn Baker** and six great-grandchildren (**Kyle Baker, Quinton and Trevon Lewis, Xander and Chloe Lewis and Brookelynn Baker**).

Part IV

On to Unionville

1945 – 1972

Chapter 13
Unionville – My Early Memories
By C.L. Judd

In 1946 or '47 I owned a '46 Ford that I had bought from **John Ryals** just after the war. I was going out west of town on a call (out where **Johnny Dixon** lives now) and a man and his wife lived there and raised some kind of chickens with a fancy topknot on their heads. I don't know what you called them, but I dropped over a little hill and the road was full of those little chickens. I guess someone had spilled some grain or something and they were all eating in the road. I was fortunate to get only one rooster out of the deal, so I stopped and I thought I'd be a Good Samaritan and go up to the house and take the rooster and maybe they could dress it. I knocked on the door holding that rooster when this old fellow came to the door. He was shaving and his face was all lathered up and a razor was in his hand. I told him I'd run over one of his chickens and I thought perhaps he'd like to dress it and I'd be glad to pay him for it. He became all excited about his fancy chicken and the lather began to dry on his face and little bubbles started flying in all directions. He said, "I'll let you pay me $1.50 for that rooster". I paid him and left the rooster but I don't know why because I just bought him. I'll never forget how mad that old fellow was at me and he ranted and raved but I had to get on to see my patient so I left, but after that he became one of my patients and was good and loyal until the day he expired a few years later.

Another time this fellow had run a nail in his eye. It was coming a horrible snowstorm and blizzard and this was before they kept the roads cleaned out and it must have been 1947 or '48. We went by way of the Novinger road because I was taking him to see Dr. Atterberry, an eye doctor in Kirksville. Going through Novinger was closer than the usual route and that's why we were going that way. I had an old jeep and it was snowing inside about as much as it was outside. We had a horrible trip but we never did get stuck. I had his head all wrapped up with soft cotton around the eye and the nail because the nail was still in the eye. I was afraid to pull it out because it would cause more damage. I'll never forget that trip. We finally got there and put him in the hospital. He lost the sight in that eye but he came out of it and was otherwise healthy.

We had a night watchman back in the 1940's who was a little eccentric and sometimes he'd drink a little on the job. He'd pull some mighty funny things during those times. He was in the old beer joint in the Staples Hotel sitting at the bar when someone yelled, "Why don't you try playing some Russian roulette"? The watchman said O.K. and he took all the shells out of his gun and held it up to the side of his head and pulled the trigger. It snapped and nothing happened so he did it the second time and nothing happened. He spun it again and did it for the third time and just as he pulled the trigger he turned the barrel straight up. It's a good thing he did because the gun went off, right to the side of his head. There was a sleeping room just above the bar and that bullet went right through the ceiling and there was a fellow asleep up there. He had his clothes and personal belonging (watch, change, etc.) on a chair and the bullet went up through that chair and just scattered stuff everywhere. He grabbed his clothes and took off and wondered what in the world was going on around there. The night watchman had powder burns all over the side of his head and his ear was starting to swell up and he couldn't hear anything because of the loud noise from the gun.

Penny Shultz, now **Penny Blue**, lived up in the northwest part of town and she had a couple of neighbors by the names of **Hod Holmes** and **Pearl Holmes** that lived by themselves. They were bachelors at that time but Hod did finally get married. Pearl was out in the garden one day hoeing and he was leaned over and his pants were stretched pretty tight. Penny had a BB gun so someone suggested that she take a pop at the seat of Pearl's pants. I guess he let out a war hoop you could hear for miles around. Penny disappeared from around there for quite a little while. She was afraid of what might happen.

Zode Burns, the brother of **Hade Burns**, lived southeast of Unionville. He was having a heart attack and it was pouring rain. It had rained for a day or two and the creeks were out and that was before there were any hard surfaced roads. Hade said he would go with me and we'd try to get down to Zode because his wife said he was having a lot of pain and was awfully sick. We took off and went to Hartford and then south. We went down across the bottom and the creek was out over the road. There were no banisters on the bridge that went over that little creek down by the Burns School house and I wasn't very anxious to cross that bridge because I couldn't see the floor. We were guessing where the road was by the fence posts and we finally could see with the headlights. The water was making a kind of ripple going over the south side of the bridge and I knew where the bridge was then, if there was a floor there. So I eased the jeep up to it and it went upon the floor and we went on across. I'm telling you I was petrified and Hade was too but Zode was so sick we decided that we'd better get to him. We went on in the house and he was perspiring profusely and hurting in the chest, so I listened to his heart and I gave him a shot real quick to ease the pain. He was swearing up a storm and so after he eased a little I wanted to check his pressure and check him over a little more. We were trying to get his underwear sleeve up (he had huge arms) and we were having quite a struggle. He was pulling and pulling and he said, "The damned New Deal, every since the Democrats have been in office, I haven't been able to find any underwear big enough for me. Doc, (that was the first time I had ever seen the man) I don't give a damn what your politics are but I'll tell you right now, I'm sure not a New Dealer!" I got a charge out of that and after Zode got calmed down and feeling better, I said, "Well, I guess we've done about all we can do Hade. I believe he's going to be much better now". We'd already stayed an hour or two when Hade asked, "Doc, do you have anything you have to get home for before daylight?" And I said, "Not that I know of Hade". He said, "Well, let's just stay all night. They've got a bedroom upstairs, let's just go up there and go to bed awhile and then go home as soon as it gets good and daylight. I don't like crossing that bridge in the dark". I agreed with him. Mrs. Burns fixed us a nice breakfast and we took out for Hartford in the morning. When we got out there the creek had gone down enough so we could see the floor of the bridge and that made us feel much better.

There used to be the old Ranch House restaurant and bar that sat out by the sale barn at the junction of 136 and highway 5 south. I could have almost survived on the Saturday night work I got out of the Ranch House suturing up the people that got knifed and hurt and cut in some of their famous brawls. I distinctly remember suturing up one man three times in one Saturday night. A fellow came in to the hospital about 9:00 pm and he had quite a gash on his abdomen. He'd been knifed and it was almost a perfect appendectomy incision. I sewed that all up and he said he was going back to the Ranch House and get that SOB that did this to him. He took off and in about 30 minutes here came the next fellow in and he did get him. He's been knifed in the abdomen and around his ribs, and this man said, "I'm going to go get the SOB that did this!" I said to him, "Why don't you fellows just call a truce and forget it, I'd like to get a little sleep here". His reply was, "Naw, I'm going to get him!" So he went back and in a little while this same fellow that I had just stitched up was back. By then I had sutured one guy once and the other guy twice. After I had sutured for a long time I said, "You're surely not going to go back out there are you?" I figured it was about closing time by then. He said he was going to go home and this was the man who ran the old Staples Hotel at the time and so he went there. Long about 4:00 am, I'd just gotten into bed, when the phone rang. The nurses called me and said to come back up that they had **Murl Bags** to suture up. I thought, "Again, I've worked on him twice already tonight!" and they said, "He's in here again and he's been cut again." So I went back down there but it wasn't the same fellow who had worked him over this time. It was someone down at the Hotel that had worked him over. I got him all sutured up and finally got home to bed.

66

Another time a fellow was brought in who had his throat cut from ear to ear. The cut was clear down to the carotid artery and the jugular vein but it hadn't gone through them. You could see them pulsating in his throat. Also he had been cut on both wrists. The radial artery and tendons had been cut. He was the bartender at the Ranch House. Someone knifed him with a big long knife and I sutured on him for hours. He survived but because of his asthma and emphysema he didn't live too many more months.

Ed Christy ran the hotel in downtown Unionville and one evening someone came into the old hotel to get a room and asked Mr. Christy if he had hot and cold running water. His reply was, "You betcha, all you've got to do is ring your buzzer and I'll run right up with a hot tea kettle full of water". He had many, many sayings and we sure got a kick out of the things he did and said.

Back in 1948 I had a New York Chrysler when one of my patients became very ill. I was taking him to Kirksville to the hospital because there wasn't much ambulance hauling back then so I put him in the back seat of my car and his father was in the front seat with me. His mother was in the back seat with the patient. Those old New York Chryslers would run faster than they should and I was going down the road a little faster than I should have been and we got down just to the edge of Novinger when an old man in a Model T Ford, (without a top on it and a little bed on the backend where he'd sawed the back seat off) came off the side road and took off across the road in front of us. We took him broadside and I mean we scattered things. That old Model T flew in all directions and he went up in the air and landed in a muddy ditch on the right side of the road. We got stopped and I jumped out and ran back up the road because none of us were hurt. He was just getting up and wiping mud off of him and I asked, "Are you hurt Mr.?" He answered, "No, I don't think I am but what happened? Did the old T explode?" And I said, "No, I hit you." He said he never did see us and that he thought the Model T just exploded. What was fortunate was that he wasn't killed and no one in my car was hurt.

In 1949 I was going to Kansas City to a postgraduate course. I had a 1949 black Cadillac and when I got to Kansas City I went down

Troost Avenue and turned right on 14ᵗʰ Street and went over three or four blocks to go up Baltimore to the old Dixon Hotel which was just across the street from the Muelbauch. When I pulled up to this street, there went two or three Cadillacs along there that looked just like mine. I thought something funny was going on. When the stop sign said go I turned and cut right in between the cars and I looked back and there was some guy going right through the stop sign behind me. I thought, "Well, what am I into now?" But they happened to be going the same way I was and we went on over to Baltimore and turned right (a one-way street). The lead Cadillac pulled off at the Muelbauch Hotel and I had to stop in the line of traffic. I couldn't figure out what was going on but come to find out, **Harry Truman**, the United States President was being escorted to the hotel. Mr. Truman had a penthouse he stayed in when he came back to Kansas City. So they unloaded him and the secret police came to my car and they gave me the third degree. They wanted to know what I was doing in the parade and I said I didn't know. I had just turned and I was in it and I couldn't get out. I had to prove my credentials and show them every card I had in my billfold. Finally they let me loose and I just went across the street to the Dixon Hotel. That was quite an experience and I thought they were going to throw me in jail before it was over.

In the 1950's we had a store down at the east end of town which everyone called 'Little Chicago'. A lot of people rented rooms in little cabins all around there and a certain fellow that stayed down there got into an argument with his girlfriend and he decided that he was going to commit suicide (at least that's what he told her). So he got some blank cartridges and put them into his .38 and he got some red cake coloring and put in a capsule to hold in his mouth. Right in front of her he whipped out this .38 and shot, apparently right through his heart. He dropped to the floor and bit down on that capsule. The red cake coloring started running out of his mouth making it look like blood and of course it scared all of them to death. They called for me to come down there because they'd had a suicide and they also called the sheriff but I beat him to the scene. I went in and there he was on his back, gun at his side and this red cake coloring running out of his mouth. Somehow it looked kind of suspicious and I stooped over

68

to take his pulse. The pulse was better than mine and so I noticed a powder burn on his shirt right over his heart. I ripped the shirt open and found there was no blood coming from a wound. There was just a skin burn from the blank cartridge. His pupils were reacting normally and everything else was just fine. About that time the sheriff arrived and he said, "It looks like he got it done this time". My response was, "No he didn't. He's going to have to do a better job than this. If he wants to do it, why don't you give him a shell out of your gun that really works? I'm going back up to the office and get to work. Until he can do a better job than this it isn't a coroners job". The sheriff said, "I guess I'll go with you and maybe he'll decide to do it right some of these days". He never tried that trick again.

Other coroner cases included two murder cases down in Sullivan County and several more in Putnam County. Of course, the airplane crash of 1962 was the most significant event of my coroner's career. A Boeing 707 crashed north of town and all aboard were killed except for one man who lived a short time. (You can read more about the plane crash in chapter 24).

There was a taxi driver in Unionville in the 1950's by the name of **Hazen Ackley**. Hazen was amusing to listen to and sometimes his imagination got away from him but still everybody liked him. He used to tell the story about a shotgun he had. He said it would reach out farther than any shotgun he's ever heard of or seen. He said he went out to the lake during duck and goose season and was sitting in the blind and nothing had come in and he looked up in the sky way high and he said, "There went a bunch of geese". He said he shot up into the air and then put the shotgun across his lap and was just about to go to sleep when 'plop" a big Mallard 'goose' fell in front of him. That old shotgun had reached away up there and got him and brought him down. Of course I don't know if anyone had ever heard of a Mallard 'goose' before.

Another story that Hazen used to tell was about where he was raised, which was at his grandparent's place. It was about 200 yards from the house to the barn and he said he made himself a slingshot and he said he was really accurate with it. Whenever he got hungry he'd step out the kitchen door and there'd be some pigeons out on the roof of the barn. He said he'd let loose with that slingshot and plop, a pigeon would fall off the roof and he'd run out and get it and bring it to the house and his grandma would make pigeon pot pie for him.

Russell Johnson worked at the Kozy Korner filling station and he always had 'loafers' all night because it was the only all night station for miles around. There was this one particular fellow that would get drunk and come in there and sleep behind the stove and when morning would come Russell would get him up and send him home. This drunk had been in the pen for writing bad checks and Russell was an artist at imitating handwriting. He'd see your handwriting and imitate it and make you think you had done it. He was just that good. So while this particular fellow was asleep, Russell said, "I know how to have some fun with him. I'll just write out a check to the Kozy Korner and sign his name like he does and I'll ask him about it when he comes to if he does. I'll ask him if this check is good to send through the bank. Of course he didn't have any money in the bank so sure enough when he sort of roused up Russell asked him, "Say, what about this check you gave me a couple of days ago? I was ready to send it to the bank and I didn't know whether you wanted me to or whether you wanted to make it good." The fellow looked at the check and thought he had written it and he replied, "Oh my God, don't send it to the bank. I don't have any money in there and I'll go back to the pen for sure if I give another bad check." Several days later Russell told the fellow it was just a prank.

We had a sheriff in Unionville by the name of **Bub Berry**. He was quite a man before he became ill. He had been a sergeant in the army and he was pretty rough, I mean, he could take care of himself. We had a fellow that came to town about every Saturday night and got drunk and would get into trouble. Bub tried to be good to him and cooperate with him and let him go home without putting him in jail and things like that, which he didn't seem to appreciate. One night I was up to the Kozy Korner and Russell Johnson saw the fellow come in and he asked, "You seen Bub Berry? I'd like to whip him." Russell said he was there about 15 minutes ago and was on his way home. It was getting along in the night and Russell said he would call Bub and tell him the fellow wanted to whip him and see if he wanted to come back. This fellow said O.K. and he let out an oath and said to call the so-and-so and get him up there so he could give him a good whippin'. So Russell called him and Bub said, "You tell him to wait right there and that he'd leave his gun and badge at home. Sure enough Bub drove up, got out of his car and looked at this fellow and said, "I understand that you want to whip me?" The fellow said, "I sure do!" With that he reared away back and was going to swing a long haymaker at him and while he was making that wild swing Bub slipped in on him with a short punch and hit him under the chin and knocked him cold. He just fell back on the pavement and there he was when Bub picked up a bucket of water that was there to fill radiators and threw it all over him. With that Bub went home and that was the end of the fight. Bub was fast with his dukes and he had a short punch he could just paralyze you with.

One time in 1959, **Bill Davis** and I were coming home from a Macon football game. I had a '59 Corvette and of course there was no limit to how fast you could drive back then. We got just north of Kirksville and some young fellow went around us and he must have had his Ford really souped up because he'd pass us and then slow down and I'd pass him and then he'd speed up and pass us again. Finally we got away up almost to the Lancaster Junction and I passed him and we had to get up to about 110-115 MPH to get around him. I just kept agoin' and he kept a chasin' us and so I slowed up enough for him to go around me and make him think he was out running me and I just stayed right on him. We went that way for two or three miles and it wasn't long before the smoke rolled out of the exhaust pipe on that Ford and he pulled over on the shoulder. He'd shelled the motor out and really ruined it evidently. When he started slowing down we did too and we pulled right up to the side of him and said we were sorry and was there anything we could do for him. Bill asked if he wanted us to make a call someplace for someone to go and get them and he swore at us and said to get on out of there. He said he'd had all of us he wanted so we just took off.

When we ran the old hospital, we had a maintenance lady who cleaned the floors, fired the furnace and so on. She was a very capable individual. One day another lady came up to the hospital to see her brother who was a patient there. She had the misfortune of developing diarrhea while she was up there so she just politely started running down the stairway, down the hall, and all the way out to her car with her bowels moving all the way. Someone called the cleanup lady to come and take care of the mess. She'd mop a little and then she'd swear a little until she was through with her clean up job. Then she proclaimed, "You tell that old lady that if she comes back here and that ever happens to her again to for goodness sake please stand still."

There was a fellow by the name of **Ralph Leach** who lived over by the golf links. **Ike Fowler** was the night marshal at that time and it was just before the 4th of July. I had been down to the old hospital and I came down by there. Ike was out in the street and he asked if I had any Cherry Bombs. Of course, now they are outlawed, but then we used them and they made a lot of noise. We went over by Ralph's and Ike lit a Cherry Bomb with his cigar and threw it in the yard. We took off and sure enough when we got to town, the red light was on over the city hall. (That was before the dial system was in effect). The central office had a signal that if someone wanted Ike, they could flip a switch and that would turn a light on at the city hall over the door. **Mary Thompson** was the telephone operator and she put the call through for Ike. Ralph was on the line and was yelling, "Get over here quick, somebody just shot through my house." We got in Ike's car and went over to Ralph's. We looked all around while Ralph told us the wild tales of someone shooting up his house. Ike said it was all quiet and that if it happened again to call him. We went back to town in Ike's car and got into my car and went back out to Ralph's and Ike lit another Cherry Bomb and threw it into the yard. We took off for town again. Sure enough, the light was on again and we went in and called Mary. It was Ralph and he said that they were shooting at him again and they were going to kill him. We got back into Ike's car and went over there and listened while Ralph told us how the bullets were whizzing by his head and all that stuff and tried to show us in the wall where the bullets had landed. The old house was so beat up that no one could really tell what had happened. It wasn't too nice of us to do that but it did change our nightly routine and create a little excitement.

Another character, **Doug Hill**, had a problem with drinking the spirits. In 1959 I had a Corvette and I would leave the top down and at night when it got cool I'd wear a leather jacket. This particular night I had stopped by **Jim Dover's** DX Station to fill up with gas and announced that I was going to Worthington on a call. Doug heard me and he jumped in the Corvette and said, "I'm going with you Doc." I said O.K. but you may get real chilly. We took off and got down east of town and those Corvettes would wind up tight. It had a 140 MPH speedometer on it and I think it would just about do it. We got started across that bottom just west of Hartford and I opened 're up and got it to about 120 MPH. Doug started to yell, "Oh God, we're going too fast, I'm freezing to death". It had a big tachometer on it right beside the speedometer and Doug looked at that tachometer which said 55 (that's 5500 revolutions per minute). Doug exclaimed, "Hell, we're going faster than that aren't we?" and I said, "Look at this Doug". I had to yell because of the wind. He looked over and saw that the speedometer was laying on 120 MPH and boy he sobered up in a hurry. He just started screaming and yelling so I slowed 'er down a little and got down to Worthington where the call was to a little house on the southeast corner of the square. Just north of that Richmond's had a beer joint. So I told Doug that when I came out from the call that he had better still be in the car or I would leave him. "I'll be right here he said", Well, I knew he wouldn't because when he saw that beer sign up there I knew he'd go over to the establishment. Sure enough, when I came out of the house, Doug was gone. I went up to the beer joint and there he was and he'd already had two bottles of beer and didn't have any money. I bailed him out because I knew if I'd left him down there they'd lynch me the next time I came back to town. I paid for his beer and got him out of there but he never did offer to go with me anymore after that trip. I told him, "Doug this alcohol is going to kill you". He would drink everything from rubbing alcohol to vanilla extract and I told him the alcohol and the poison was going to kill him. He said, "Hell Doc, there's a lot more old drunks than there are old doctors".

When **Pearl Smith** was night watchman he had a sarcoma (a type of cancer) in the spine. He was a gentleman and a dear friend of mine. He kept working and working just as long as he could. I was giving him medicine for pain because he did have a lot of that and I had the privilege of hauling him home the last night he worked. It was snowing and I had been on a call east of Unionville in the jeep and I came in and went by city hall where I saw him lying on a table. He lived up at the west end of town and he walked back and forth to work. He said that he hadn't turned off the lights around town yet that night and I told him I could do that for him. I drove that jeep right up onto the sidewalks and I could reach right out the door and shut the lights off all the way around the square. I expect that some of the people wondered why jeep tracks went around the square but they probably had a good idea who it was. Anyway, after I got the lights all turned off, I loaded Pearl in and took him home and that was his last night to work. He was such a wonderful person and his wife was a grand lady. They had a great family and their children are still friends of mine and were patients until I retired. I delivered grandchildren for them and I can't say enough good things about the Smith family.

There was a lady who had a harelip and a cleft palate and it was a little hard to understand her. Of course this would sound a little better on tape than it will look on paper because you can't imitate her method of speech on paper. Anyway, she came into the office and she had some hemorrhoids and I gave her some suppositories for them and I thought I had gone to great lengths to explain to her how to use them. I thought everything was O.K. and I told her to do it three times a day. So the next afternoon after two tries at this deal she called me and said, "Doc, do you know those are the hardest pills to swallow that I ever did see. I'd put them on my tongue and they'd stick and then I'd try to swallow and I'd gag and throw them back up. I worked hard at it and finally got two of them down but my God they're hard to swallow." I almost fell out of my chair with laughter and disgust and so forth.

A number of years ago this elderly lady had a little old feisty dog and I sat down in a chair and tried to examine her and that dog just wouldn't leave me alone. He'd hop up in my lap, lick my face, and I'd shove him out and back he'd come and that went on the whole time I was there. I hardly could take care of my patient. I gave her a shot and some medicine and she said she'd go in the bedroom and get the money for me. This dog got right up in my lap again and licked me in the face and I had an alcohol sponge in my hand that I was using to rub the ladies arm before I gave her the shot, so I just politely dobbed that dog under the tail with that sponge and boy he got off of my lap and started scooting across the rug pullin' himself when the lady came back in the room. She said, "My, my, old Ring has got the worms again. I'll have to go down to **Don Herrick's** drugstore and get him some worm medicine. That kept him out of my face but I was kind of sorry that I caused him to have to have a dose of worm medicine when he probably didn't have worms.

July 3, 1973 **Dr. Phillip Brackett,** who was here for seven years before going to Memphis, Missouri, had a lot of antique clocks and he wanted me to sleep in his house while he was out of town for a day or two so no one would break in and steal his clocks. It came up an awful storm that night, the night before the opening of the centennial in Pollock, where I was to give a speech there the next morning. The wind started blowing real hard and I was just sleeping in my under shorts. I ran to the front door and out to see what was going on with it storming and pouring down rain. The door slammed shut right behind me and there I was locked out of the house, on his front porch, in a horrible rainstorm, in my under shorts. I didn't know what I was going to do; however, there wasn't anyone out on the streets, so I took off running the two blocks to the hospital in that pouring rain. I went in the back door and dashed down the hall and into the doctor's lounge without any of the help seeing me. I put on a surgical scrub suit, went out and asked if they had a key to Dr. Brackett's house and went back there. It could have been an embarrassing situation if someone would have been around to see me but thank goodness they weren't.

There was a suicide out west of town and the fellow had been dead several hours. The family thought he had probably shot himself the night before and he was lying in the front yard. I had been coroner in Putnam County for over forty years at that time and **Danny Peto** was the Sheriff. He called and said that he would pick me up and take me out to where the man lay. As we were driving out of town Danny opened that big LTD Ford with the big engine in it up and got up to a speed of nearly 100 MPH. I said, "Danny, I don't really see any sense in this since I've never been on time to a coroner's case yet, so just slow this thing down. We had a lot of cases that were very interesting and Danny was always on the job and did his work well. The kids always liked him and he had a way with the young folks. He could always win them over and help them because they didn't seem to get upset when he was reprimanding them but he could get them to do what was right. **Danny** is a good friend and he and **Pauline** were so good to me all the time I was in the hospital in Kirksville and after I went to Lee's Summit. I can't tell you here the great things he did for me but it helped so much. In fact I'll never forget and never be able to repay them for all the kind things that they have done.

In 1978 we had our National Osteopathic Convention in Hawaii and over 400 doctors and their families from Missouri flew over on the same Boeing 747. We had a great time over there and on the way back, out over the Pacific about two hours from Los Angeles, we lost an engine and I was sitting over the right wing and could see the twin engines on the right side. They had worked on this one engine for quite awhile before we left Hawaii and we were late getting off. I saw it catch fire and I supposed they had a way of extinguishing it. Everyone was having a great time on the plane and they were whopping it up at the bar, movies were going and I saw the flight engineer come back through the plane after this one engine went out. It wasn't but a minute or two until he came on the speaker and announced that we had lost this end of the motors on the right wing and that we couldn't gain altitude with that motor gone but that we could maintain the altitude we had. He said not to worry that they were going to get permission from LA to come straight in because of the inability to climb. They assured us that everything was well and good and we'd stop in LA and get the plane repaired. Everything got so quiet you could hear a pin drop. They closed the bars and the movies were shut down. It was the longest two hours I think I ever spent. Near the coast we could see out and there were red lights going everywhere at the airport. When we got low enough we could see that they had foamed the runway and that there were fire trucks and ambulances on either side of the runway. They told us to buckle our seat belts up tight and lean over and keep our heads between our knees during the landing. We made an uneventful landing and just as soon as the wheels let down and we started taxiing there was great clapping and hollering on the plane. Everyone was mighty glad to be back on the ground again. They wouldn't let us off the plane and we sat there another two hours while they fixed the engine and then we flew on to Dallas/Fort Worth and caught another plane into Kansas City. That was quite an experience and gives you time to think about things and wonder if you were ever going to get home. Someone asked me why they had us put our heads between our knees and I replied, "I didn't know but I found out. You could fill your pants a lot easier if you were leaning forward than if you were sitting straight up."

I never can say enough about **Bill Davis** and his family. We have been great friends for years and years. They've always been so good to me and I've always tried to be good to them. When I had my heart attack in 1984 Bill had already been set up for by-pass surgery so I wasn't able to go with him when he had his surgery. But when I had my surgery in 1988 he was right down in Kansas City with me and stayed there. I didn't realize it, I was so sick I hardly knew he was there. But everyone told me he was and there were so many other people from around Unionville and Pollock who came to see me. These included **Ed Dooley**, the Christian Church Minister, Leo **Bruce**, **Mel Casto**, the **Schoonovers**, **Kenneth Tipton**, **Jean Fowler**, **David and Hazelee Fowler**, and many others came and some sent flowers, and this and that and I don't think they will ever know how much I appreciated those things. I know I'm missing people and I'm sorry. My ex-wife, **Ruth Judd**, who lives in Lee's Summit close to our daughter, was so good to me at the time I was ill. She stayed in the hospital with me so much and **Serece**, who was just out of the hospital with brain surgery, would come with her but couldn't stay for long periods of time. The entire family was very good to me including my nephew, **James B Judd**, and his mother, **Mary Judd**. My sister, **Ruth Moss**, and my brother, **Claude Judd**, from Arizona, called all the time. **Mabel Judd**, my sister-in-law in Newtown called and my son-in-law, **Bill Lewis**, was at the hospital almost every day to check on me and confer with the doctors. If it hadn't been for **Bill** and **Ruth** I could have died a couple of times when the nursing staff was unaware of what was going on with my condition.

Chapter 14
Abduction of a Doctor

This section is taken from an article that appeared in the Unionville Republican January 1948

Dr. C.L. Judd was abducted and robbed on an all night ride as he was made to drive his own car over many roads to Kahoka, Missouri.

Last Wednesday night Dr. Judd was whisked away from the Monroe Hospital, taken on an all night ride and robbed of $400 in cash.

(Apparently without intention Dad played directly into the hands of his abductors and became the victim in a thrilling bit of melodrama.)

As a matter of routine he had filled his gas tank about seven o'clock and then parked to the west end of the parking lot on the north side of the hospital. He pocketed the keys and went into the hospital for a little over an hour. He called Mom and told her he had one more town call to make and then he would be home. He opened the door of his car, slid into the seat and adjusted the key. The car is equipped with a lighting system, which turns the lights on as the door is opened, but this had gone out of commission and the interior remained dark.

He stepped on the starter and the engine was in motion so he backed the car to the east. As he paused he felt a hard object in his back and the words, "Get Going." Surprised, he immediately thought someone was playing a joke on him and he asked, "What's going on, what's the joke?" The hard object punched his ribs, the voice commanded that he get going and not turn around. The hard object he took to be a gun, and by that time he was convinced there was no joke in the situation.

He drove west and turned north by the Lowry Miller Lumber Company, then back east on No. 4. As he drove he saw **Dolphus Haigler** cross in front of him, and he said he felt himself wishing some sort of accident would occur. He slowed, but the voice repeated, "Get Going." Only one man issued instructions, and he later determined there were two of them, but one never spoke loudly enough for him to hear.

He was directed to drive to the Glenwood Junction, then to Exline, Centerville and Bloomfield, Iowa, and then to Kirksville, Missouri. At the Pig Stand, north of the city limits, Dad was told to drive back to Lancaster, then to Memphis and on east to Kahoka. Before getting out of the car, the men demanded that Dad give them his billfold, which he did.

This was about 4:00 am Thursday morning and Dad drove back to Unionville even though the gas gauge on the car showed empty when he arrived.

He immediately went to the City Hall, where **George Bailey** was on duty, and there he related his story. Bailey called Kirksville, to notify the Highway Patrol, and although they investigated, there never was an arrest in the case.

The men never searched him, he said, and seldom exchanged words, but confined themselves to giving directions by only one man, (who was the same in every case). Dad had no opportunity to see the faces of the men, and they kept him looking straight ahead. He said he saw many people walking about on the streets of Lancaster as they went though the first time, but that on his return from Kahoka he saw no place open except a small lunch stand at the edge of Memphis.

(Dad was not harmed in any way, but he admits that he was thoroughly frightened, and kept wondering what would be the outcome of it all. When released, his only thought was to get home as quickly as possible.)

Chapter 15
The Old Staples Hotel

Ed Christy operated the old Staples Hotel and drove a taxi in Unionville. He was another interesting character in town with whom Dad enjoyed sharing tales with and about.

The hotel stood where the Farmer's Bank parking lot is today. During the depression, Mr. Christy would rent the third floor rooms for $1.00, the second floor rooms for $2.00 and the first floor rooms for $3.00 per night. The building was getting old and the mice and rats were beginning to take over the place. Two ladies came through town one night and rented a third floor room. The next morning, when they got ready to leave, they started complaining about the rats and mice fighting all night and they could not sleep. Ed leaned back and replied, "What do you expect for $1.00? A bull fight!"

Television sets were just appearing in the rural areas in the late 1940's even though there was only one station. This station was from Ames, Iowa, over 100 miles away. Ed decided to purchase one of these sets, so **Mutt Rouse** and **Forrest Hoyt** arrived to install it for the Christys. Ed's wife was not very happy about the whole thing and she commented to Ed, "We can't afford that set and besides we won't be able to see anything half the time." She continued to stay on his case while the dealers went back to the shop to get the tower and antenna. When they returned Ed met them on the porch and said, "Fellows, this is a damn good set you sold me. We don't even have the antenna up yet and I am already getting hell!"

During a spell of real hot weather many people were stopping by the hotel to get a cold drink from Ed's old glass water cooler. A salesman happened by and asked Mr. Christy how he was doing. To this Ed replied, "I'm trading cold water for urine and selling postage stamps at cost. You can sure get rich doing that."

Chapter 16
Fire Alarm

One morning following a tonsillectomy at Monroe Hospital, a funny incident happened. In the late 1940's and early 1950's doctors used open drip ether and a suction machine to keep the blood out of the throat. Also a jar with a hose running from it was hooked in the mouth of the patient. This was how the ether was used to keep the patient asleep during a surgery. This procedure was employed because if they didn't do it this way, the patient was liable to wake up during surgery and they couldn't give the patients ether without the mask over their face.

After the tonsillectomy was over, there was some ether left in the jar on the machine. One of the nurses took the jar and poured the either that was left into the stool in the nearby bathroom. Another nurse, **Bea Lykins**, went in to use the bathroom and she was smoking. She sat down on the stool, and when she had finished her cigarette, she dropped it between her legs into the bowl. There was a loud BOOM! The explosion scared Bea so much that she came running out of that bathroom ninety to nothing, fanning her fanny with both hands and screaming bloody murder.

She wasn't hurt, but needless to say, everyone involved learned a valuable lesson.

Chapter 17
The Case of the Missing Fork

One afternoon back in 1951 the sheriff brought in a so-called tramp. Someone had called him down to Livonia to see this man who seemed to have some kind of troubles. This fellow was in a park down east of town, and he was complaining of severe abdominal pain. He was trying to vomit, and he really was complaining of pain when they brought him into the clinic in Unionville.

When Dad asked the man what his problem was he replied, "I swallowed a fork". Dad thought this was a bit amusing so he asked, "Pitch fork or table fork?" With that the man got mad and proclaimed, "Damn it! I swallowed a fork! I've got a table fork in my stomach! Give me a shot or something for the pain!"

Dad's first impression was that the fellow was lying, and that he was an addict and just wanted some morphine. Morphine was about the only thing doctors had in the way of narcotics in those days. Dad rolled up his sleeves and looked at the man's arms but he didn't see any evidence of needle marks or anything else, so he put the fellow on the X-ray table. Lo and behold, there was a table fork in that man's stomach. When questioned, "How in the world did you get that down in your stomach?" the fellow answered, "I used to be in a side show in a carnival and I swallowed rubber, collapsible forks at that time. I thought I'd try it with a regular fork because I told a bunch of kids in the park that I could do it. They actually got a fork for me to swallow.

I stretched out on my back and opened my mouth and sure enough, it went on down into my stomach and it's killing me!"

Dad couldn't doubt the fellow after seeing the X-ray. He called **Dr. Gillum** from his office on the square to bring some ether and they put the man to sleep, opened him up, and got the fork out. The old fellow healed up and they let him go in about 10 days. Of course, neither doctor got any compensation on that one.

Chapter 18
The Polio Epidemic Hits Putnam County

The 1940's through 1954 presented a real challenge for the doctors and nurses across the country because there was a big epidemic of polio. The first nation-wide trial for mass vaccinations against the poliovirus wasn't to be until 1955. Some people died and many more were crippled for life after those epidemics. Even President Franklin Roosevelt was afflicted and spent many years in a wheelchair.

When a person gets sick with the polio virus the body can become paralyzed because of the damage to the nerves and spinal cord and these cells cannot repair themselves. If there was enough damage, the person would have to use crutches, wear braces, or even be limited to a wheelchair in order to move around.

There was more than one type of virus that caused polio. Another type of virus caused what was called bulbar polio, which affected the brain stem and interfered with certain controlled functions, like breathing. People died suddenly with that type of polio or they had to be put in iron lungs (automatic breathing machines) in order to survive. In order to properly diagnose bulbar polio it was necessary to perform a spinal tap. Symptoms of bulbar polio included high fevers, headaches and a stiff neck. Symptoms of paralytic polio were similar but with a weakening in an arm or leg, causing the limb to remain small and the patient would limp or not be able to raise their arm. Anyone who had these symptoms needed to be checked out, and because a spinal tap was not a procedure that could be done at home, the patients were sent to Laughlin Hospital in Kirksville where **Dr. Grace Sawyer** and a team of physicians and nurses had set up an area in the lower level of the hospital called the polio ward. The patients diagnosed with the disease were given high doses of Vitamin C, which boosted their immune system. They were treated with hot towel packs and exercises several times a day. This was how the Osteopathic doctors worked with the patients and they had a much better success rate than conventional treatments seemed to achieve.

I remember the night I came down with the symptoms of polio. I was spending the night at my **Aunt Mary** and **Uncle Rollo's** place at the flower shop house on Main Street. I was sleeping in the bed with **Barbara** and **Olga**, my cousins, and in another bed in the same big attic room were their brothers, **Herman** and **Charles**. Willie had graduated the spring before, and was away in the air force. Luckily none of them caught the virus from me that night. My fever went very high and I was so dizzy I felt like I was falling all the time. Aunt Mary wrapped me up and put me in a trunk they had used to move from Hawaii. It was full of towels and bedding and that comforted my falling feeling. The next morning Dad took me to Kirksville and there I stayed for several weeks in Laughlin Hospital. They had a special ward set up for polio patients and I remember my bed was next to that of **Jennifer Shelton**'s and near by was another classmate, **Larry Gadberry**. We took large doses of vitamin C and they packed us in hot towels several times a day to sweat the fever out of us. There was also the physical and water therapy as a part of our recovery treatment. Back home people were worried and many public meetings were called off, the movie theater and swimming pool was closed at times and many people were affected.

Other people I remember coming down with polio were **Linda Stewart** (**Galloway**), **Selena Darrah**, **Janice Fowler**, (now **Doolin**) **Elsie Lunsford** and her daughter, **Karen** (now **White**). I visited with Elsie and Karen the other day and they could remember having terrible headaches and Karen remembered the awful enemas they gave us to clean out our systems. Elsie remembered that her older daughter

Marilyn and her friend **Donna Parish** (now **Neighbors**) were not allowed to go to school because they had been around Karen when she came down with polio.

Even though the cases were transferred to Kirksville, these were Dad's patients and he took special interest and concern for them. I remember one incident where Dad was transporting a young patient, along with her mother, to Kirksville, and they were in a serious car accident. A man turned his car around in the middle of the road, just south of the Lancaster Junction. It was later determined that he was intoxicated. The child wasn't hurt, and I don't remember the injuries to the mother, but I do remember Dad being in the hospital several days with broken ribs, a broken nose, and many bumps and bruises. There were no seat belts in cars in those days.

Two years after the most serious outbreak of polio in Unionville, Dr. Jonas Salk developed a vaccine to immunize all against the disease. I was in the 5th grade when they lined all the kids up in the lower hall of the elementary school and gave us the shots. There were no sugar cubes or liquid drops at that time so we all had to endure the shots. Even though I had the disease, there were two more strains of the virus, so I still had to take the shots.

Now, fifty some years later, the world is protected from that frightening and life- threatening disease known as poliomyelitis.

Chapter 19
Babies, Babies, Babies

One of Dad's first OB cases, after moving to Unionville, was with a family in Hartford, Missouri. **John** and **Mabel Carmen** already had five children and Dad eventually delivered 11 more for them. John was a character, if there ever was one. Dad arrived early in the morning, and while he waited, he watched John feed some hogs that were across the lane. He was watching intently when John said, "Get your damned eyes off those hogs, I'm goin' to pay you!" He was always saying something witty like that, and yes, he always paid for Dad's services.

Another family for which Dad delivered 11 children was the **Grover Robbins** family.

Often it was difficult to get to homes way out on the county roads. Dad always said the only difference between a jeep and a mule is that a jeep is slightly warmer and a little faster. The comfort of the two was about the same. On one occasion, Dad was called about 25 miles southeast of Unionville on a night the mud was really rolling. He took the old jeep and put it in plow gear. After he left the highway, he still had several miles to go before he got to the farmhouse where he delivered a healthy baby. About three months later, he had a call to the same place to deliver another baby. When questioned, the reply came, "It's my step-daughter this time." Dad proceeded to load up the old jeep and go out on the back roads in order to deliver another baby. Once the baby was in the world, he laid the birth certificate out. He filled in the mother's name and hesitated by the father's name. The stepfather reared back and announced, "By God! I'm the father! If those two don't give a damn then who should?" Dad got a real astounded look on his face, but he filled out the birth certificate and headed back to town.

One birth that made Dad a little more nervous than some of the others was when I was born. That little piece of drama took place at the Monroe Hospital on January 18, 1944 with Dr. McDonald the primary physician, Dad assisting and Bea Lykins as the attending nurse. Of course, Mom really did all the work on that one. Mom and I stayed in the hospital for 10 days, and I'm told the nurses carried me around whenever they had time and so I felt loved from the very early days.

The following story relates something that occurred in 1948 before the old hospital was remodeled. A woman was hanging out clothes in her seventh month of pregnancy and she took a sudden pain. They brought her in to the hospital where it was discovered that the uterus had ruptured and she was hemorrhaging inside. It just so happened that **Dr. Cecil Wise** was in the hospital, having just delivered another baby, so he was handy to give the anesthetic. The patient was prepared for a caesarian to try to keep her from dying from the hemorrhage and shock. After Dr. Wise got her to sleep, Dad opened up the abdomen. Blood and amniotic fluid ran out of the incision, down the side of the table, down under the table and right into an open 220 socket that was in the old operating room. There was an awful noise, a kind of zzzzzzzzzzzzzzzzit. Dad backed up, looked under the table and saw fire shooting out of the open plug. Immediately he stuck his foot over the plug and the fire burned a hole through the sole of his shoe before the fuses blew out. After that they were trying to finish up a surgery without any lights, so the nurses got flashlights and held them so the surgery could be finished. Thank God the patient lived but the twins she carried were dead before the abdomen was opened. Dr. Wise had bet $5 when they were scrubbing for surgery that the patient would never come off the table alive. After he got her to sleep, he added a steak dinner to that bet. He never did pay off that debt, but that was all right because everyone was happy to have a live patient.

Back in the 1940's a drug salesman was in the office one evening when Dad got a call to go out and deliver a baby. This Sharp and Dohme salesman was a real nice looking fellow, and he always dressed immaculately, so Dad asked him to go along while he delivered a baby. The salesman remarked that he had always wanted to see a baby being born. The family had several children, and when Dad and the salesman arrived, the wood-burning cook stove was already going with boiling water for the occasion. Dad introduced the salesman as Dr. Head. Everything went according to plans, and after the baby was born, Dad wrapped him in a blanket and handed the baby to the salesman. He said, "Here Doctor, you go clean up the baby." The salesman looked kind of funny, but he was a good sport, so he took the baby into the kitchen. When Dad was finished with the mother, he went into the kitchen to help, and the salesman said, "You so and so, what did you do that for? I don't know anything about cleaning up babies." He always swore he would get even with Dad, but the occasion never did arise.

On another occasion in the old hospital, Dad had a senior medical student working with him. A patient, who already had a whole covey of babies before this one, went into labor. It was always very difficult to get her to go to bed when it was time for her to deliver because she would walk the floor until the last minute, have the baby, and then go into the bathroom to clean it up. Dad had told her that one of these days she was going to have a baby while she was standing. To this she replied, "I know more about this than you do. I've had more babies than you have." Dad knew that this time she was about ready to deliver, but she wouldn't get in bed, so he told the student doctor, **Dr. Ron Herrin**, to keep a close eye on her and try to get her to go to bed. Dr. Herrin began tagging her up and down the hall like a little puppy dog. When she would have a pain, she would stop and he'd stand behind her and wait. Finally she had a real hard pain and exclaimed, "Oh, it's on its way, the baby is coming out!" Dr. Herrin was screaming, "Dr. Judd, come quick, we've got an emergency here!" But it wasn't an emergency as far as Dad was concerned for he knew everything would be all right. They took the lady and her baby back to the bed before they cut the umbilical cord. The perspiration was just rolling off Dr. Herrin's forehead when it was all over, and Dad commented, "Well, that was a good experience wasn't it?"

Another incident that happened was when Dad was way out in the country delivering a baby. This girl was at her mother's home and they had a big family. There were several grandchildren, all who had been born at home. The mother was always with her children when they delivered their children. The baby was born and Dad took it into the kitchen to clean it up and dress it when he heard this terrible commotion in the bedroom. The patient was just sneezing as hard as she could, one right after another. Dad ran into the room and asked, "What in the world is making that woman sneeze like that?" Her mother, standing there said, "I put pepper up her nose." And Dad said, "Pepper, up her nose, why?" Her reply was, "So she'd sneeze that afterbirth out. I always did that when I helped with a baby."

In 1942 Dad was delivering a baby out in the country. The older children had been sent to a neighbor's house, and there wasn't anyone at home except the expectant mother and father. The mother wasn't progressing very fast, but all of a sudden she let out a scream, and the baby came with that one pain. Dad didn't realize that there was a dog under the bed, and when the lady gave out the loud scream it must have scared the dog. The dog jumped from under the bed and clamped down on Dad's ankle. At this very moment, the father fainted dead away on the floor. There stood Dad, holding the baby up with both hands, shaking a dog off his ankle, and looking at the unconscious husband on the floor.

OVER 3500 BABIES

When **John Carman's** wife was about to deliver her twelfth baby, John began to have doubts as to how he would handle such a big family. He made the statement that if his wife got pregnant again he was going to commit suicide. Sure enough she did get pregnant again, and John tells the following story:

> "I went to the barn, threw a rope up over the rafters, tied the rope around my neck and stood up on a barrel. When I was just about ready to kick the barrel out from under me a thought came to me. Wait a minute, I thought. I could just be hanging an innocent man!"

Milford and **Bernadine Crouse** lived on a farm about 12 miles southwest of Unionville. There was no electricity at the farm, and it was an extra warm August day in 1945. Bernadine was in labor, and when Dad got to the farm he could see that it was going to be too hot for her to continue her labor in the house. A bed was put under

95

a shade tree in the yard, and it was there that she continued her labor until after dark. When it got too dark to see, a few lanterns were hung in the tree. Eventually, **Carolyn Crouse**, now **Grimes**, was born. Her mother hemorrhaged and Dad had to rush back to Unionville and pick up some plasma to give to Bernadine. That was just one of many home deliveries that Dad made before electricity was installed in the rural areas.

Dad made his last home delivery in 1957. The rest of the babies were born at the Monroe Hospital until the Putnam County Hospital opened in 1963. Dad delivered three generations for a few families, and in many instances, he had delivered both parents of a new baby.

On October 16, 1986 Dad delivered his last baby. **Dr. Casady** and his wife **Linda** had their second daughter, **Nicole Elizabeth**, early that October morning. He was scheduled to deliver their first daughter, **Jennifer**, who was born August 3, 1984 but she came along just a couple of weeks after Dad's first heart attack, so Dr. Casady was on his own for that one. Well, Linda really did all the work.

The last baby story is not about human babies, but about baby pigs. **Elton Webb** had a sow that was about to deliver, and he couldn't find the veterinarian. Elton and his friend, **Neal Cullor**, appeared at our house for help. Pigs were bringing a high price at the market in those days, so Dad knew how important this was to Elton. He went by the hospital and picked up some instruments and some real heavy sutures. They went out to the barn, which was the old icehouse, just across the highway north of the Country Club. Neal held a bucket that had been stuffed with chloroform-saturated cotton over the sow's head. Soon she went to sleep and Dad proceeded to cut her open. He took out the baby pigs, sutured the sow back together and everyone was pleased, if not surprised, that mother and babies all survived the ordeal.

Chapter 20
Birth Control in the 1950's

Maybe one of the reasons Dad delivered so many babies during his practice was because birth control options were limited in the early years of his practice. There were no pills, so the options were: a couple could abstain, use foam, spermicidal jelly, or withdraw. Most of these methods didn't work and were very unsatisfying. The best methods in those days were barriers, such as condoms or diaphragms. They both ruined the mood of the moment, and the only place to buy condoms was at the drug store where they were kept in a drawer behind the counter. The men were too embarrassed to ask a female clerk, so they waited for a male, most often the pharmacist. The condoms would be wrapped in a plain brown wrapper and handed to the customer. It's so different today where condoms are passed out at school or advertised on television or available in many different stores and service stations. Women didn't like diaphragms very well, because it meant interrupting the love making to insert it, which took away the spontaneity. The only successful methods of birth control were tubal ligation or a vasectomy. If a woman had a C-section, this could be done at the same time. Otherwise, it took a more involved surgical procedure, unlike today where they can do the procedure laproscopically. A vasectomy was a much simpler procedure and much cheaper.

In 1954 there were an increasing number of men in the prime of life that were asking their doctors for what they called 'the operation'.

Before World War II this operation was done mostly for a sterilization method for the insane. Five out of six of the men asking for the operation in the 1950's were married and either didn't want to have any more children or thought their wives would be put in danger to become pregnant again. They knew the operation was simpler and cheaper for men than for women. Some family doctors would do the operation in their own offices, but others preferred them to be sent to a urologist. The operation took about 20 minutes and cost about $25.

After birth control pills were introduced, Dad always said an aspirin worked just as well as the pill and was much cheaper. He said it was all in how you used the aspirin. His method was to just put the pill between your knees and hold it tight there.

Chapter 21
On Being a Doctor's Daughter

*While in high school I took a speech class with **Miss Bertha Bell McClaskey** and I wrote the following speech for her class my senior year.*

It took a while for me to realize the difference between my family and that of most other families. My awakening came one time when I asked my mother why daddy was always going to other people's homes. Her answer, " It's all right dear, you're father isn't an ordinary man, - he's a doctor".

Doctors are a breed apart, as my father often proved.

Doctors' households have no problem about teenagers' monopolizing the telephone. Long before adolescence sets in, the doctor's child knows that the telephone belongs to Daddy. It must never be used unnecessarily. When it is used, the conversation must be brief. The common thing to say is "I'm sorry but I must hang up. Father is expecting a call." The doctor's child also learns how to take a message. Before you're old enough to go to school, you know how to take the caller's name and number, to ask the nature of the complaint, and to get the information referred to in medical homes as TPR (temperature, pulse and respiration).

Teachers seemed to have an unshakable belief that doctor's children were extraordinarily healthy. If I missed school, the teacher would eye Mother's note suspiciously and say, "You were sick? A doctor's daughter?" Actually, nobody gets sick as often as doctors and their families. For no matter what the epidemic raging, or how virulent the germs and viruses going around, doctors are busy sticking their faces into infected throats, being breathed on by feverish patients, coming home exhausted and bearing the day's invisible harvest of germs. If there's anything "going around" it's sure to be going around a doctor's household.

But when doctor's families get sick, the treatment usually is a strictly do-it-yourself procedure, one reason being that your father is seldom home. Dad had a lot of medical textbooks with articles, illustrating in detailed color photographs a victim's appearance. That's how a doctor's wife diagnosed their children's illnesses. Once Mother got my disease tagged, all she had to do was read what the book prescribed and then call my father to bring it home from the office.

In serious illnesses it is an unwritten rule of the medical fraternity that, because of possible emotional involvements, a physician does not treat his own family, nor does he charge a colleague for medical services rendered. This automatically makes doctors families the least sought-after patients on the face of this germ-ridden earth. Yet much as every doctor hates to be called to another doctor's house, even more, because of the reflection on his skill, does he hate seeing someone else called instead. Years of professional relationships hang while the doctor and his wife debate which colleague would be offended if he weren't called, and which would be inconvenienced if he were called. The usual result is that no doctor is called.

This makes me recall the night when I felt miserably ill, and as a well-indoctrinated doctor's daughter, I tried to struggle through the night on my own, letting nature take its course. I tried to figure out what was wrong but couldn't, and so at 3:00 am with the situation completely out of control, I found no way of avoiding the emergency of bothering Dad.

Both parents came quickly and held a bedside conference. Mother asked, "Should we take her to the hospital?" To this Father scowled. "You mean wake a doctor at 3:00am.? Mother leaned over the bed and asked if I could possibly wait until 7:00 or 8:00. How many times had people called Dad in the middle of the night, but no, we couldn't bother a doctor at this hour. If I could only get to sleep . . . . The next morning I was on my way to Kirksville with a case of bulbar polio. By all odds I should have died . . . any ordinary daughter would have. But I was a doctor's offspring, over whom heaven must keep special watch . . .

Nine times out of ten, the prescription for the patient who lives in a doctor's house is aspirin and bed rest. For more potent medication there's a wonderful institution known as the "sample drawer". Pharmaceutical houses send a multitude of samples to doctors, and most of them go into the sample drawer awaiting the day of need. It is from this drawer that the family ills were treated.

This, of course, imposes something of a problem, for it was necessary for us to match our ailments to the medicines available in the drawer.

Once while cleaning out the sample drawer I picked up an unfamiliar bottle of huge, green pills. "What's this?" I asked. Dad took the bottle, read the label and handed it back. "Take one," he said, "It will probably be good for you."

There's no sport in the world that can hold a candle to being a doctor's daughter if you like to live dangerously. Statisticians may not have figured the mortality rate among physicians' offspring, but I'll wager this is one segment of the population in which the jungle law of survival of the fittest holds good. A doctor's child has to be fit to survive.

Chapter 22
My Memories of Growing Up in Unionville
1946 – 1962

My earliest memories of life in Unionville include playing with my cousins and the Herrick kids on Main Street in front of Edmunds' Flower Shop. The shop was in a house one half block west of where the Dairy Lane is today. My mother's brother, **Rollo Edmunds** and his wife, **Mary**, along with their five children, **Wilburt, Barbara, Herman, Charles** and **Olga,** lived in that house on Main Street. They had moved to town in 1949 after living in Hawaii for 15 years.

Rollo and Mary helped run the flower shop for four years. I remember spending many nights there while Mom and Aunt Mary worked all night arranging flowers for funerals, weddings, proms and so forth. Uncle Rollo made stilts out of boards for us to walk on and we always had a game of hopscotch drawn out on the sidewalk if we weren't roller-skating or playing Monopoly.

I even remember when the trains went through town right past the Kozy Korner and behind the **Pittman, McCalment** and **Herrick** houses near Main Street.

There was a very special lady named **Nellie Montgomery**, who lived next door to **Abe Bonebright**'s grocery store. She was my babysitter until I was old enough to go to school. She had an icebox, not a refrigerator, and I remember the ice truck coming by every few days and bringing a big chunk of ice and putting it in the box. The man would give the kids some ice chips to chew on and we were excited on those days. Other times **Gummy**, as we called her, had us sit and practice writing cursive, making curves and circles, filling up page after page in our special writing pads. People tell me today that I have a pretty handwriting and I'm sure it was because of her instruction.

Another thing I remember about her place was the nights I stayed all night with her. We would lie in bed and listen to the radio until I fell asleep. I think the programs were Fibber Magee and Molly and One Man's Family. Sometimes we heard The Lone Ranger. Other kids I remember staying there were **Geri Ann Armstrong**, who moved to Milan and **Julia Lowry,** who later lived in Princeton.

We lived in a two story white house on west Main Street located where the Hy -Vee store stands today. We lived there from 1948 until 1956 when I was in the 6th grade. On weekends our neighbor, Shirley Crump and I went with another neighbor, **Jerry Godfrey**, to **Orin Lee Halley's** pony farm to feed, play with, and ride the ponies. Jerry was **Valda**'s father Valda was Orin Lee's wife). Kathy Imboden (now Pfaff) and I stayed all night at the Godfrey farm and experienced farm life with no electricity, no indoor bathroom, and no running water. The Shetland ponies on the farm were fun, but they could be very mean. I remember one time when Kathy got bucked off a feisty little pony and they were always biting us. I loved my neighbors on West Main and the ones I remember most were the **Bernackers,** the **Darrahs**, the **Davis'**, the **Mahoneys**, the **Godfreys**, the **Crumps** and farther west were the **McCalments** and the **McDonald**s. To the east a few houses were the **Forbes** and **Valee** and **Haden Burns**. I remember riding my bike up to Valee's many times because she had beautiful flowers and she gave me jelly bread whenever I wanted it.

Our house seemed big to me and for several years there were two apartments upstairs. **Delsie McKinley** lived in one as long as I could remember and **Ab and Lois Bonebright** lived in the other apartment. Because they lived in our house, I thought they were part of our family. My bedroom was just inside the front door and to the right through large French doors (the room must have been a parlor at one time).

Straight ahead from the front door was a long staircase (at least to a 6-year-old it seemed long) going up to the apartments. My cousin, **Barbara Edmunds**, would regularly baby sit with me. One night we were asleep in my room when Ab came home upset and a little drunk, wielding a gun and threatening to kill Lois. He came right in the front door and past the bedroom where Barbara and I were sleeping. Barbara heard it all while I slept soundly. Soon after that Lois and Ab moved out leaving an empty apartment upstairs. That apartment became my private playroom. I spent hours up there with my paper doll families. I cut out clothes, set up churches and stores from books I carefully picked out at Ben Franklin's 5 and 10 cent store on the north side of the square, which was owned by Ed and Marie Schick. When they didn't have the exact pieces of clothes or furniture I needed, I got out the Sears catalog and cut out things to use. This arrangement was great because upstairs, in the empty rooms, I didn't have to put things away when I finished, but just left it set up for the next day.

Delsie McKinley's apartment was a place I liked to play also. She would color with me and tell me stories. I remember her popcorn with candy syrup on it. She worked at the telephone office and later for Mom at her flower shop and dress shop. When we moved to the house south of town, Delsie moved into an apartment on the town square above **Pickering**'s Barber Shop

I always felt bad because I didn't have a sister so I 'adopted' many friends for sisters, and today several of my 'young' friends are very much a part of my life. For this I give credit to the Unionville all school reunions, cell phones and email. Now that our families are grown and on their own (except we are all involved with many, many grandkids) we all get together as much as possible. **Sharon Herrick Link, Kathy Imboden Pfaff, Carolyn Cooley Aspegren, Carol Grabosh Stark, Mary Taylor Michaels, Jane Streeter Andrews, Sharon Lowe Steele, Donna Cooper Snyder, Deloris McHenry Jarman,** and **Pat Frick Jennings** keep in touch several times a year either by phone, email, or in person, living all the way from Unionville to Arizona. Even some of the guys keep in touch regularly: **Mick Mitchell, Ron Stuckey, Orval Spence** and **John Ed Rhodes** to name a few. I probably left someone out but I didn't mean to. Others like **Jim Dover, Don Fowler and Ed Rhoades** are at all the reunions.

During the time we lived in the big white house on Main Street, I remember being quarantined twice. Once for scarlet fever and once for some other contagious diseases I acquired from the germs Dad brought home. Those were the days before many of the vaccines we have today had been discovered. I experienced three kinds of measles, mumps, chickenpox, whooping cough, scarlet fever and even polio.

Elementary school was held in a two-level building just two blocks north of the town square. There were seven classrooms on the upper level for first through seventh grade. The lower level of the school building contained the restrooms, cafeteria, auditorium and special education classes. A child had to be six years old before January 1 to start school in the fall. Because my birthday and Ron Stuckey's birthdays were both January 18 we had to wait until we were six and one-half before we could start school.

Miss **Gladys Gillum** was our first grade teacher. The thing I remember the most about that year was the time she lined us all up and as she sat in a chair in the middle of the room we all filed by and got a spanking for talking too much.

Our second grade teacher was Mrs**. Pauline Calhoun,** and she would give us colored strips of paper each day we were good, and if we had four strips by Friday we got to have an extra recess. Another memorable thing she did was have us put our heads down on our desks after lunch while she read to us. My favorite book was the _Boxcar Children_ and I dreamed I had a family like that. I still like to read those books to my grandchildren. I really credit Mrs. Calhoun with teaching us to read and spell better than later classes because she didn't go with the new methods but taught us phonics. Today the schools, again, realize the importance of phonics.

I don't remember much about third grade since that was the year I was sick all the time and missed a lot of school. Along with several other students there was some time spent in the hospital with polio.

Miss **Sylvia Jones** was our teacher and she was very kind and helpful, and even though I missed many days, I still passed to fourth grade.

In fourth grade, with Mrs. **Earlene Webber**, I found out I had to get glasses. Dad said my bad eyesight was probably due to all my high fevers the year before.

Our fifth grade year we had **Ruth Morris** (Miss Ruth) for a teacher. She was very young but we didn't know that, and she was lots of fun because she played with us on the playground.

Mrs. **Faye Hill** taught us many things in sixth grade. For one thing, she was an artist, and she had us do several projects including working with pottery clay and making vases and dishes that I still have today. Also she had us spend several weeks using our 'other' name. It was then that I learned everyone's full name and I still remember most of them to this day: Mary Jeanette, Carolyn Sue, Ronald Lee, Sharon Lynn, Carol Valee, Katherine Ann to name a few. Miss Faye's husband, **Mortimer Hill**, was our rural mail carrier and he would sometimes let me ride with him on his route. He drove an old Model A Ford and it was lots of fun.

By the time we got to seventh grade we had our first men teachers – **Mr. Ross and Mr. Whitworth.**

In summary, the best parts of grade school were:

Roller-skating

Sledding down the big hill to the ball diamonds

Playing softball and dodge ball

Jump rope where two people turned the rope and everyone lined up to jump on their turn

Going to Franklin Childs' store a block south of the school and having bologna sandwiches for lunch and picking out penny candy.

Franklin and his wife were so patient as each of us picked "one of those, two of those, and one of those". Then they'd put them in little white bags for us and off we'd go back to the playground with our treasures.

One of my favorite activities at home was the get-togethers with Mom's friends to make candy for Christmas gifts. They all gave each other special hair treatments, like cuts and permanents. **Delsie McKinley**, **Evelyn Rennells**, **Flossie Mullenix**, **Irene Comstock** and probably others I can't recall would work way into the night beating candy until it was just right to pour and set. My job was mostly to lick the bowls clean when they finished. When I got my hair permed I would set on piles of Dad's medical books (which I still have today) and when I was waiting for the next step to process I'd look at the pictures in the books. That was really an education. I don't think I saw a normal naked body until I was an adult.

I learned to play the piano as a young girl by taking lessons from Mrs. **Marie Schick**. She was so patient and kind with all of her students. After the Christian Church got it's new organ from the **Summers** family, she taught us to play hymns, and on Sunday morning one of her students would play the organ and she would play the piano (or visa versa) along with them. It was a great way to learn how to play in church.

It's hard to believe now that we felt like the most privileged kids in the world even without television, air conditioning, cell phones, computers, gas grills, microwave ovens or power lawn mowers. There were no Wal-Mart's or McDonalds and the only pizza available was home made from a Chef Boy Ardee box. Our special drink was Kool Aide (lots of sugar) because no one had soda pop at home, except on very special occasions. Our transportation was skates, bikes, and our two feet, but we didn't mind at all as long as we could get together with our friends. When we were old enough to drive, our cars were without power windows, power steering or seat belts and we didn't really have to be too careful about the speed limits out in the country, since there weren't very many law officers in the county. As a result, too many kids and adults had to pay the ultimate price.

By the time we got to high school we were busy with sports, music, and all the things teenagers find most important. Some of our fondest memories include:

- Girl's bunk parties at anyone's house.
- Drinking cokes and playing the juke box music at **Bailey's Café**
- Hanging out at the Country Club, swimming and playing golf
- Going to the movies three times a week (that's how often a new show came in, Saturday night, Sunday afternoon and Wednesday night.
- In the summer we went to the **Sky-View Drive In** where **Myron Woolever** tried to watch over us so we didn't get into much trouble.
- Driving from one end of Main Street (from the Tastee Freeze) to the other end (by the Country Club) and honking at everyone you met. We'd even park on the square once or twice during the evening and visit with all the other cruisers
- Bridge parties were popular at the time. This was where several people pulled their cars up to both ends of a bridge, on a dark country road, turned on the radios to the same station and danced on the bridge.
- Probably the most dangerous thing we did was ride a sled (or tire, shovel or car hood) which was pulled behind someone's car or truck after a snowstorm.

It seems like I was never home or at least never home alone. I was either staying all night with one of my many friends or they were at my house. It was fun to ride the school bus out to the home of **Sharon Lowe** and **Mary Joyce Cook** to spend the night. More often than not you could find me at one of the homes of **Rebecca Riley**, **Carol Grabosch**, **Pat Frick**, **Sharon Herrick** or **Kathy Imboden** any night of the week.

During our years from age 12 to 18 Rainbow Girls played an important part in our development. It was there that I learned to memorize long passages including many scriptures from the Bible. We learned how to be ladies in dress and actions, and how to sit without crossing our legs or even our ankles. **Dad and Mom Morgan (Keith and Grace)** spent many hours working with the girls in our community, and we were all better prepared for life because of their efforts. We knew how to speak and how to use our best manners.

When I was in the 8th grade my mother purchased a Vibraharp for me to play, and I had to go to Kansas City (a three hour drive) on Saturdays to take lessons. We would arrive in the city around 9:00 am and Mom would spend her time buying flowers for her shop back home. I would take a taxi from downtown Kansas City to 41st and Main, where the Conservatory of Music was located. I would take a Vibraharp lesson, attend a music theory class, and after that I would walk several blocks north on Main to Luyben Music where I also took a clarinet lesson. Mom would pick me up there and we would travel back home arriving around 6:00 pm. That made for a very long day every other Saturday. To make the trips more interesting for me, I would often take a friend along. Several times we would spend the night and go to a play, a show or even the circus. When I got old enough to drive, I would drive myself on this trip and take a different friend each time. When my girlfriends were not available to go, my 'little buddy' **Jerry Jarman** was always willing and able to go along. One time we were being pursued by a bunch of boys in a fancy car on the dual highway through Liberty when a highway patrolman pulled us all over. I remember Jerry and I trembling in our boots as we waited to see what was going to happen. Jerry knew we didn't have any money and he thought we were going to be put in jail. The trooper asked us if those boys were scaring us and when we said, " yes", he let us go (with a warning to SLOW DOWN) and he kept the boys. A few years ago a trooper in our area, who became pretty high up on the force, celebrated his retirement. His name was C.E. Fisher and I remembered he was the one who stopped us that day. I will never forget staring at his name badge as we waited for the verdict. All of us felt very grown up doing such a daring thing as to drive to and through Kansas City, but I had done it so many times it just seemed natural. Needless to say, after all those music lessons, Mom was quite disappointed when I decided to become a science teacher after I went to college.

Our senior year in high school found us taking our senior trip to Rockaway Beach on Lake Taneycomo in southern Missouri. We spent several fun-filled days there, boating, skiing and just hanging out. We will never forget the trip home as we listened to the bus' radio and heard of the commercial plane crash just north of Unionville. Some people on the trip lived near where the plane went down and wondered if it was on their land. (See Continental Flight 11 in Chapter 24).

Fourth Grade Valentines Day Play

A few members of the class of 1962 at their 30th class reunion in 1992.

Chapter 23
Monroe Hospital

On February 19, 1939, there was an open house attended by some 800 guests when the Monroe Hospital and Clinic opened their doors. The hospital and clinic served Unionville and the surrounding areas for twenty five years.

The hospital's first patient was Mr. **Clare Magee** who entered the facility on February 12, 1939.

The hospital staff included **Dr. J.H. Martin, Dr. E.L. Brown, Dr. L.W. McDonald** and **Dr. Pearl Hart. Dr. C.L. Judd** joined the staff in 1940. **Mrs. Maude Liveszey** was bookkeeper and receptionist, and later **Wilma Cullom** joined the group as bookkeeper and receptionist.

Dr. G.G. Gray became a member of the staff in the summer of 1962, just before the hospital closed.

After the first patient, Clare Magee, in 1939, there were 17,333 patients that were hospitalized at the Monroe Hospital. The last patient to be admitted was **George Ray Clinkenbeard**.

Dad, Dr. McDonald and Dr. Gray continued to have office hours at the Monroe Clinic until a new clinic could be built.

I have great memories from the days at the Monroe Hospital. When my parents needed a babysitter, I often was left at the hospital with the wonderful teenage nurses who lived and worked at the hospital when they were in high school. I can remember sitting at the nurse's station on the second floor of the building and twisting cotton on the end of sticks to make cotton swabs. We would also cut gauze into 4" X 4" squares that were used during surgery. Supplies didn't come in sterile packages like they do today, so after these supplies were ready, they were wrapped in paper and autoclaved for sterilization. Instruments and glass syringes were boiled in a kettle or pressurized in something that was like a canner. Infections never occurred from contamination in the hospital.

I had the pleasure to sit down with **Gloria Mills** and **Glenda Rhoads** who started working as nurses in 1951 and continued off and on until the Hospital closed in 1963. They then worked at the new hospital. Gloria and Glenda are twins and they still live on the family farm, which is west of Lemons, Missouri. The ladies were very helpful in jogging my memory about people and situations at the hospital. They reminded me that some of the nurses were **Sarah Beth Lemen, Bessie Runcimen, Patty Twitchell, Thelma Dye, Leone Hawkins, Betty Patterson, Zephra Newell, Myrtle Gaddis, Goldie Smith, Bea Lykins, Evelyn Steele, Edna Minear, Letha Hines, Virginia Smith, Virginia Seaton, Geraldine Hunt, Leota Johnson, Kathleen Shipley, Lucy Abbott, Roma Gillespie. Wilma Morris, Pat Kelly and Mary Alice Butler.** I'm sure we left someone out, but not intentionally.

The ladies also remembered a lot of the procedures and policies of the hospital. They noted there were a lot of surgeries performed, including removal of tonsils, appendix, and gallbladders, as well as C-sections and hysterectomies. Fingers and thumbs were sewn back on and many lacerations were sewn back together.

IV's had to be run manually with a clamp and titrated to so many drips/minute. If the patient turned their arm wrong or laid on it in their sleep, it would change the flow, so these devises had to be monitored regularly to prevent problems. There were very few antibiotics, but they remembered penicillin (used mostly for pneumonia) and later came streptomycin, chloromycetinm and sulfadiazol.

If needed, whole blood was donated or shipped from Kirksville on the day of surgery, but more often they kept plasma in the storeroom and it was given to bring patients out of shock.

In the early 1950's the nurses were paid $12.50/week along with room and board. By the time the hospital closed, in 1963, they were making $22.50/week with room and board. The nurses' rooms were on the third floor of the hospital (probably a real fire trap since there were no sprinklers and only one way out) and there were three rooms up there with room for 5 girls. I spent nights up there when I stayed at the hospital. There was no bathroom up there so the girls had to make their way down a narrow, steep flight of stairs to the only bathroom on the patient floor, which was located across from the nurses station. In those days there were no bathrooms in the patients rooms, and they didn't let you get up and walk around much so you know what that meant – the dreaded bedpan.

Three or four nurses worked the day shift from 7:00 am until 3:00 pm. Two nurses worked from 3:00 pm. until 11:00 pm and only one nurse worked the 11:00 p.m. until 7:00 am shift. Those were the days when the nurses gave the patients full baths everyday, changed their sheets everyday, and gave them good back rubs every night. When I was a patient there during my junior year in high school, I felt like I was in a vacation paradise (except for being sick).

One of the nurses, Goldie Smith, was deaf and she taught me how to sign all the letters of the alphabet. She was very sweet and kind and such an efficient worker.

Wilma Morris, Evelyn Steele, Bessie Runciman, Letha Putnam, Gloria Mills 1951

To keep the hospital running, they not only needed nurses and doctors, but they need cooks and housekeepers. **Charlie** and **Anna Lorence** and **Lois Buckalew** were housekeepers that I remember. The cooks were **Edith Corbin, Leta Jones, Maude Gilstrap** and **Vada Houston.**

Bessie Runciman, Lucy Abbot, Goldie Smith, Patty Patterson, Wilma Cullom

The lower level of the hospital was where the Clinic was located, and there were a couple of large rooms that served as the waiting rooms for Dad and Dr. McDonald. **Dr. R.H. McCalment** also had his dentist office in the clinic. I was born at the hospital January 18, 1944 and to everyone's surprise I had my two lower teeth already. So on my second day of life here on earth I was taken to Dr. McCalment's office to make sure they were my real baby teeth. They were! I found out some years later that my Uncle Jim, Dad's oldest brother, was also born with two teeth.

Dr. Judd, Goldie Smith, Bessie Runciman, Dr. McDonald

Twelve patients were transferred from the Monroe Hospital to the new Putnam County Memorial Hospital October 13, 1963. Husted and Comstock ambulances were used to move the patients and without one mishap.

The distinction of being the first patient in the new hospital went to **Mrs. Flossie Yount**, who was convalescing with a broken left leg. The four ambulances and their attendants ran a shuttle service between the two institutions, starting at 9:30 am that Sunday morning, and they finished an hour and a half later when the last patient, **Mrs. Isa Judd**, my grandmother and Dad's mother, was transferred.

Other patients transferred that day were: **Frances Vestal, Nancy Probasco, Pete Rice, Roy Wallace, Rose Viar, George Ray Clinkenbeard, Bernitta Davis, Edna Hinerman, Sylvia Minear, Todd Arnold** and **Dan Drury**. Three patients were entered later in the day; **Mrs. Nell McWuary, Mr. Marion Houston,** and **Mr. Billy E. Pauley**.

The patients ate breakfast in Monroe Hospital and dinner in the new Putnam County Memorial Hospital. The patients were made ready for the transfer as soon after breakfast as possible. **Mrs. Barbara Thompson, R.N. Leone Hawkins, Gloria Rhoads, Glenda Mills, Goldie Smith, Lucy Abbott,** and **Patty Jo Twitchell** all helped to make the transfer.

In the early days of Dad's medical practice he had no nurses or secretaries and, of course, there were no cell phones, pagers, message machines, and no email and text messaging. Because Dad was seldom in one place, people kept track of his where abouts and reported to those in need. He said his best secretaries were the phone operators. They took messages and gave them to him as they caught up with him at someone's home. When we were in Pollock **Mrs. McDonald** would baby-sit with me when my parents went on house calls and I'd sit on her lap as she pulled plugs and connected one family to another through the wires. Dad said **Mrs. Annie McIntire** was one of the best at keeping track of his calls. When I was in grade school in Unionville, **Delsie McKinley** and **Mary Thompson** worked at the telephone office and all I had to do was pick up the phone and ask whoever answered if they'd heard from my Dad lately. Most often they knew where he was or could track him down in only a few minutes.

Chapter 24
Continental Flight 11 – May 22, 1962

No one in the Unionville High School Class of 1962 will ever forget the plane crash near there on May 22, 1962. We had spent several fun filled days at Rockaway Beach in the Ozarks for our senior trip. As we traveled home on the big yellow school bus we were listening to the radio when the news came on about the crash. A 707 Boeing jet, owned by Continental Airlines, had crashed in a field just north of town. The plane exploded in the air from what was later discovered to be a dynamite blast in which 45 people lost their lives.

In an article written by Andrea Lorenz in the Kansas City Star on January 8, 2006, she described what happened that fateful night. Although many of her facts forty-four years after the event were not accurate, I will relate some of the truths that she presented.

It was May in the Midwest and a strong storm was coming in as flight 11 left Chicago on its way to Kansas City. This caused Captain Fred Gray to fly the plane at a higher altitude than normal, 29,000 feet. As the captain started the decent coming closer to Kansas City the controller there saw a blip on his radar screen and then the object disappeared. It was 9:17 pm. Thomas Doty of Merriam, Kansas, flight attendant, Joyce Rush, and six other passengers were sucked out of the plane at 37,000 feet as the rear of the plane was blown apart. At least one-fourth of the jet's length was missing so the nose began to pitch downward. By design all four Pratt and Whitney engines detached.

At 9:21 pm, six minutes after the last contact with air traffic control, the remains of the plane crashed into a field just six miles northwest of Unionville.

When Dewey Ballard, of the Aviation Administration in Kansas City got the call that the 707 had just disappeared, he collected a crew to fly to the area to investigate. While Ballard was getting ready, citizens in north Missouri and southern Iowa were finding remnants of the airplane on the roads and in the fields. Some were taken to the sheriff's office in Centerville, Iowa, and others were taken to Cincinnati, Iowa a small town on the Missouri-Iowa border.

Farmers in the area were awakened by the activity of traffic in the normally quiet and undisturbed countryside. **Cleo Webber, Lester Cook,** and **Terry Bunnell** knew the land well and began a search for the mysterious object they had heard the evening before. Lester and his son **Ronnie** took off across the fields about 3:00 am with flashlights in hand. They crossed fences and creeks to get to the wreckage. Terry Bunnell was doing the same thing from the opposite side of the wreckage. When they spotted the wreckage just before dawn there wasn't a sound to be heard anywhere.

As rescuers arrived they found bodies all over the area. At 5:15 am they found Takehiko Nakano, a 27 years old Japanese citizen from Chicago, who was still alive. He was responsive but went into shock as they loaded him in the ambulance and took him to the hospital in Centerville, Iowa. He died shortly thereafter from internal injuries.

A makeshift morgue was set up in John Ryals' Ford garage just east of the Methodist Church on Main Street and Dad, in his duty as coroner, was out at the crash sight just as they were loading Nakano into the ambulance. Dad said all the bodies were found in Missouri. Seven morticians worked on the bodies that were brought into Ryals' garage.

There were immediate investigations into the cause of the air disaster. At first it was believed that turbulent weather caused the plane to break apart. But soon authorities were able to determine that the cause was an explosion in the rear lavatory of the plane.

A woman in Kansas City had called authorities saying her husband had been on the plane and that she had found dynamite in the trunk of his car earlier. His name was Thomas Doty. He was an honor graduate from Westport High School and the University of Missouri. Financial ventures had not gone well for him recently and he had started drinking heavily, according to his wife. Before taking the trip to Chicago with his business partner, Geneva Fraley, he purchased a new Ford Fairlane and bought life insurance to cover the cost in case of his death. He also bought a $75,000 life insurance policy at the airport for $2.50. After the investigation was complete, none of the money was paid to his widow. She received a refund check for $12.50.

W. Mark Felt, the Chief of the Kansas City FBI office, headed up an FBI investigation. Later he became the second in command in the Washington D.C. FBI office. As Duane Crawford noted in his book "In Their Own Words" Volume II, Dad worked closely with Agent Felt. He thought Felt was a no-nonsense investigator and was methodical and thorough with his work. Agent Felt was very impressed with Dad and the Unionville Community too. The two stayed in touch with each other for many years following the accident.

After being transferred to Washington D.C. Felt was assigned to the investigation of the break-in at the Democratic National Committee Offices at the Watergate complex in 1972. Almost 30 years later, Felt finally admitted to being "Deep Throat" in the Watergate scandal. His actions caused President Nixon to resign and several of his associates to serve prison time. Felt died at age 95 on December 18, 2008.

A year after the crash of the Boeing 707 Dad reflected on the happenings. ". . . most people don't realize what takes place and what has to take place" he stated as he talked about the legal aspects of a commercial plane crash. He said it took him the entire first day to realize the extent of his responsibility as coroner since he was the man with the final word. Even the FBI men working on the case would ask him permission before proceeding with anything. Dad felt his heavy responsibility every time they said, "If it's alright with you, coroner . . . . ." Being the humble man he was, his comment was, "They've forgotten more than I'll ever know."

This tragedy was a drastic change from the ordinary duties of rural community authorities such as the county sheriff, **David Fowler**, the mayor, **Aaron Stuckey** and others who had to deal with the Federal Aviation Authority (FAA), the Central Intelligence Agency (CIA), the Federal Bureau of Investigation (FBI), the Highway Patrol, the National Guard, Continental Airline officials, a disaster squad from Iowa University, and innumerable private insurance companies.

At the crash site the bodies were numbered, wrapped and taken to the temporary morgue in Unionville. Seven bodies were spotted by helicopter within a three-mile radius of the plane. All the other bodies were found in the remains of the plane. One thing I remember is the way high school student volunteers walked hand in hand across the fields searching for the missing stewardess. A little known aspect of Dad's work with this disaster was his personal liability. The CIA wanted autopsies on every body but Dad knew he needed a ruling from the Missouri Attorney General before making a decision to proceed. A coroner can be liable for any autopsy performed without consent of the nearest relative.

The paperwork was unimaginable. Three copies of each death certificate had to be personally signed, and in some cases, insurance companies required six copies. Several phones were set up and Dad went from phone to phone as he talked with the news media and insurance personnel. His voice was on national television and he was quoted in newspapers across the country.

If you have an interest in knowing more details of the people from the area who were closely associated with the work involved with this tragedy or the locations of the wreckage and so forth, you must read the well researched and precisely written articles by **Duane Crawford** that were published in the Unionville Republican during the month of August 2001. There was a series of four articles, one each week for four weeks. Also, there is a detailed chapter in Crawford's book *"In Their Own Words" Volume II*.

Sheriff David Fowler with Continental Flight 11 May 22, 1962
Putnam County, Missouri

Chapter 25
Groundbreaking for the New Monroe Clinic

April 1964

Dr. Judd,   Dr. Gray,   Dr. McDonald

On April 16, 1964, ground was broken for the new clinic, which was to be located just west of the old hospital. It is still standing today but is for sale. The three doctors of Osteopathy, along with Dr. R.H. McCalment D.D.S., had offices in the new clinic. When completed, the building was thirty-three feet wide and ninety-two feet long. It had a twelve by twenty foot reception room projecting to the north of the main building. It was made of block construction, veneered with Indiana Bedford Stone. The dental office included two treatment rooms, a reception room and a business office. Each osteopathic doctor had a consultation and treatment room. There was also an emergency room, business office, X-ray facilities, and a medicine dispensary. The contractor for the new clinic was O.M. Wales Construction Company of Centerville, Iowa.

Monroe Clinic – built in 1964 after the closing of Monroe Hospital. It stands empty and for sale in 2009.

Part V

A Season of Change
What People Have to Say

1972 – 2004

Chapter 26
The Dark Years

1972 – 1984

The period of time between 1972 and 1984 was a very emotionally difficult time for my family and me. The old mid-life crisis took hold of Dad and, sadly, he and Mom didn't make it through that crisis together.

I'll never forget the day that Dad came to Kirksville, where my family and I were living. He told me he was going to divorce Mom. Our oldest son, Daniel, was 2 years old. Because this action was so out of Dad's character and because he really cared what his patients and friends thought of him, this situation caused him to be an emotional wreck. Within a few months we moved to Lee's Summit, MO and Dad left his practice and followed us there. He lived with us for seven months in a doublewide trailer. Mom came too, and they tried to work things out. During that time, our second son, Matthew, was born. My parents were divorced in April of 1973 and returned, separately, to Unionville. Dad was remarried by the summer of 1973 and resumed his medical practice. Mom tried to put her life back together in Unionville, but found it too difficult. So she sold her home there and moved to Lee's Summit in 1975 just days before our daughter, Suzanne was born.

For the next ten years we were not allowed in my Dad's home or were not supposed to have any contact with him. My children did not get to know their grandfather and that's part of the reason I wanted to write this book. They never knew Unionville and the many wonderful people their grandfather found so special. In order to visit Dad, we would come to town and spend 15-20 minutes with him in his office. His new wife had a daughter, who lived in Lee's Summit, only minutes from our home, and they would come there to visit her, but Dad was not allowed to call or see his family without a major upset. I felt really caught in the middle during those years, trying to protect Mom and missing my Dad.

Dad retired from his active medical practice in 1984 and just a few short weeks later he had his first major heart attack. He was just 68 years old. The recovery time was difficult and stressful, and his relationship at home was becoming more strained. **Danny Peto** was sheriff in Unionville at the time and he recognized the stressful situation that Dad was experiencing. During one particularly difficult time Danny picked Dad up as he was walking in the neighborhood, and took him immediately back to a Kirksville hospital. Dad stayed in the hospital for several weeks until one morning, very early, (about 6:30 am) we drove to Kirksville, and he met us in the lobby of the hospital. We took him home with us to Lee's Summit before anyone could stop him from leaving.

My husband's father was living with us at the time and so for the next two years we had both fathers living with us. This emotionally and physically broken man was whom my kids knew as their grandfather.

After these two years Dad gained strength and got his second divorce. He didn't truly become his old self until he returned to Unionville to live among his friends and patients.

In September of 1988, it was discovered that I had a brain tumor, larger than a tennis ball, and in less than two weeks I underwent surgery to remove that tumor. My recovery was long and I ended up missing that whole year of teaching school. By December of that year it was determined Dad would need open heart (four vessel by-pass) surgery.

Mom had never remarried and she faithfully took care of both of us during those long months. She spent many days sitting at the hospital with Dad as he battled for his life, because there were serious complications and set backs in his recovery. After several months of recovery, Dad was anxious to get back to Unionville, since he was never satisfied anywhere else in the world.

Dad had been living in the senior housing north of Main Street and near the Putnam County Hospital and he was ready to have a larger place. He bought the old Altes Feed Store building just a block west of the square. **Glen** and **Peggy Davis** had converted this building into a two-bedroom apartment. He set up housekeeping there in 1989 and remained there until his death in 2004. The front bedroom was converted into a small office and his living room was a waiting and visiting room for many patients and friends. Even after Dad married **Carolyn Smart Bomgardner** in 1997 they continued to use their home as an office. (Read more about this in Chapters 2 and 31). The door was always open and the welcome sign out to all who came.

C.L. Judd home apartment in the Altes building one block west of the town square in Unionville, Missouri from 1987 until his death in 2004.

Chapter 27
Las Vegas Fire

November 1980

Dad always seemed to be where the action was, but on November 22, 1980 that 'on the spot' presence could have proven fatal. He was staying at the MGM Hotel in Las Vegas while attending continuing medical education classes when a fire broke out. The fire started in the kitchen and thick smoke traveled through all 26 floors of the hotel quickly. Dad was always up and out early so he was not in his room when this happened in the early morning. More than 85 people were killed and 534 others were injured. Within 10 minutes the fire gutted the casino and left 10 people dead there. The flames were limited to the first two floors but most of the other people who died did so from smoke inhalation above the 20th floor as the smoke traveled instantly to the upper floors through the stairwells. Helicopters rescued some people from the roof, while others escaped along outside stairs. Authorities indicated that many of the people panicked and jumped to their death from as high as 17 floors.

Chapter 28
The Sale of Monroe Clinic

July 1, 1980

On July 1, 1980, the Monroe Clinic in Unionville became a satellite clinic of KOHC. The clinic opened in Unionville in 1964; however, Dad and **Dr. McDonald** had worked together in the original Monroe Hospital and Clinic since 1945. Dr. McDonald graduated from Kirksville College of Osteopathic Medicine in 1932 and Dad in 1940.

Employees at the clinic included: Mrs. **Kristin Tipton**, L.P.N.; Mrs. **Reva Carter**, L.P.N. and pharmacy distributor; Mrs. **Judy Valentine** and Mrs. **Melissa Pauley**, lab technicians; Mrs. **Atholene Cook**, clinical assistant; Mrs. **Maurine Lorence**, bookkeeper and insurance coordinator; Mrs. **Donna Neighbors**, receptionist and paramedic; and Mrs. **Elenora Montgomery**, housekeeping.

The facilities at the clinic in Unionville featured six treatment rooms, a laboratory and X-ray room, a pharmaceutical room, an office, a waiting room, a reception area and an employees' lounge. The doctors performed minor surgeries in the office at the clinic and they were the only doctors on staff at the hospital in Unionville.

Kirksville College of Osteopathic Medicine (KCOM) students interned at the Monroe Clinic for many years. **Kelly Smith**, KCOM senior, was completing his four-month internship when he commented on the value of the clinic to him. He said, "I learned so much. You can read a lot, but it's just not the same as being on the job."

Dr. McDonald said, "This is definitely a geriatric community with possibly 75% of our patients being senior citizens."

When questioned if he would like to continue practicing for a long time, Dad answered, "Only if mother and father will let me – Mother Nature and father time."

This was in July of 1980 and Dad saw his last patient just one month before he passed away on August 10, 2004.

In 1984 Dad announced that he would retire officially on July 1 of that year and that he would continue to see patients at the rural clinic in Newtown, MO a couple days a week for most of the year, but taking off a few months each winter to go to Sun City, Arizona. That never took place since in July of 1984 he had his first of several major heart attacks.

The following information was in an article by **Keith Dinsmore**, Unionville Republican Newspaper owner and editor:

"Dr. C.L. Judd and Dr. L.W. McDonald have agreed to sell the Monroe Clinic to Kirksville College of Osteopathic Medicine.

Dr.'s. Judd and McDonald will continue to practice at the clinic and provide health care services to the Unionville community. Several questions directed to KCOM President, Trowbridge, related to the effect of the clinic transaction on the future of the Putnam County Memorial Hospital. Occupancy at the 44-bed hospital has been below 50 percent, which is below the level usually considered necessary for efficient operation.

With the sale of the clinic, Dr. Judd and Dr. McDonald both became salaried staff members of KCOM. **Dr. Trowbridge** said that the hope was to recruit more doctors to the area and that the new doctors would receive a guaranteed salary and have an incentive program, which would provide similar rewards as a private practice.

Hospital Administrator **Myron Woolever**, said he "welcomes KCOM and hopes they will fill the communities needs." He said all they were interested in is having enough doctors to serve the hospital and the community."

Dr. Trowbridge expressed the following:

-KCOM officials share a concern for the future of the hospital since it would be difficult to attract physicians here if the hospital was not available.

-that the cost of health care would 'not necessarily' increase because of the change, while noting that the charges at the clinic are as much as 20% below others in the area;

-KCOM may be forced to discontinue operating some of its rural clinics staffed by senior students due to inadequate numbers of patients and

-physicians who would locate here will have the resources, manpower and expertise from KCOM and KOH to provide back-up services.

Dr. Judd said patients should not notice any change in the operation, adding that both he and Dr. McDonald each have two-year contracts with KCOM to continue in practice. They have an option to renew at the end of each two-year period so long as their health will permit them to practice.

Chapter 29
McDonald, Judd Named 'Citizens of the Month'

By the Putnam County Chamber of Commerce Written by Keith Dinsmore and published in the Unionville Republican in 1982

It takes a lot of cooperation and dedication for a couple of country doctors to serve a community together for 37 years. Dr. L.W. McDonald and Dr. C.L. Judd, whose combined 92 years of service to Putnam County is of legendary proportions, have worked as a team since 1945 in a spirit of dedication to local residents.

In recognition of their service, they have been named "Citizens of the Month" for January and February.

Their partnership in the Monroe Hospital and Clinic goes back to 1945, when both moved to Unionville. Dr. McDonald, known by his patients and friends as "Doc Mac", had started his practice in Powersville in 1932 (50 years ago this month) and joined with **Dr. J. Neal Martin** seven years later in establishing the Monroe Hospital.

Dr. Judd started sending patients to the hospital from his practice in Pollock by 1941 and became Dr. McDonald's partner four years later, when he purchased Dr. Martin's interest in the facility.

The old hospital, originally the Wentworth home and now the Monroe Manor, could accommodate 12 patients, and was expanded to accommodate 20 or more patients in 1947. "Doc Mac" recalls that his original partner, Dr. Martin, wanted to name the hospital after something that had been successful here. Since **E.N. Monroe** had made a name for himself with the Putnam Fadeless Dyes, they decided to name it after him. Monroe subsequently donated several thousand dollars to help equip the facility.

Although they originally contemplated only overnight stays, patient demand required that they perform their own surgery.

The two doctors recall one incident when cooperation was crucial to their survival. While performing a caesarian section on a patient, fluids ran off the operating table into an electrical outlet and blue flames shot up from the floor. While Dr. McDonald continued with the surgery, Dr. Judd placed his foot over the outlet to contain the blaze and prevent an explosion since ether was being used on the patient. By the time the patient's abdomen had been closed, a hole had been burned in the sole of Dr. Judd's shoe. Candlelight was used to help complete the surgery and the patient emerged from the operation in better condition than the doctors.

After the Putnam County Memorial Hospital was constructed in 1963, the two doctors built the new Monroe Clinic. Although they sold the facility in 1980 to the Kirksville College of Osteopathic Medicine, the two doctors remain on the staff of the clinic. The addition of **Dr. Stephen Casady** last year and the expectation of **Dr. Mark O'Brien** joining the staff on June 1 after his internship is completed here is intended to allow the two long-time physicians to take it a little easier in the years ahead. Dr. Judd recently had his 65th birthday and Dr. McDonald will be 75 next July.

Both doctors, graduates of Kirksville College of Osteopathic Medicine, have given service above and beyond the call of duty during their professional careers. They have given physicals to school children and have followed the football team for many years to be on hand in case of serious injury.

They are pleased with the results of the transfer of ownership of the clinic to KCOM, believing that it will help assure the continuity of medical service in Putnam County.

They believe that some younger physicians are willing to carry on family practices in rural communities and provide devoted service, although many have chosen to specialize in recent years. Dr. McDonald points out that there were only 15 internship opportunities for graduates in 1932 – enough for less than 10 percent of the graduates that year.

Putnam County is fortunate that these two dedicated physicians decided to practice here during their entire careers and we are happy to honor them as "Citizens of the Month".

Chapter 30
Rodger's Store in Pollock, Missouri

Virgil and Bernadean Rodgers operated the general store in Pollock, Missouri since 1945 until Virgil's death in 2005. Pollock has a population of 131 people today.

Walking in the door of the general store one would see several rows of canned goods and racks of necessities, like safety pins, sewing thread, etc. Beside the old cash register was a King James Bible. Dad traveled the 15 or so miles south of his home in Unionville to visit the Rodger's store every Thursday, where he'd buy a pound of cheddar cheese (Longhorn style), and to quote him, " It's the best flavored, smoothest tasting cheese you will ever want". Before cutting the hunk of cheese off a big round kept in an old refrigerator at the back of the store, Virgil would excuse himself; go out the back door of the store and into his house to wash his hands. When he came back he would get into the old refrigerator and pull out the round of cheese. He'd slice off a hunk, wrap it in plastic (never weighing it, he's done it so often) and collect his $3 for the pound.

On the day in 2003 when my husband, Ron, and I visited the store with my Father, all of a sudden Bernadean remembered she had cornbread in the oven and hurried back to the house, which is attached to the store, to rescue the bread. Virgil pulled out a yearbook from under the counter and talked about his time in Hawaii during Pearl Harbor. He was in the 27th Infantry Company H and it just happened

137

that he pulled K.P. duty on the day Pearl Harbor was bombed. There were only 32 out of 250 men who made it out alive from his unit. Virgil had to live with hearing impairment since the war because of the bombing.

Things hadn't changed much in the store since the 1940's and my favorite thing was a tin sign on the wall as you enter that said, "There's Not Much to See in a Small Town, But What You Hear Makes Up for It."

Virgil Rodgers cutting off a pound of cheddar cheese for Dad

Chapter 31
What the People Have to Say

The people that Dad treated as patients, and those that he just met on the streets in north central Missouri, were his life. He would rather be visiting and telling his famous stories to both young and old, than eat or sleep.

The next few pages include quotes from some of the letters sent to me in 1984 when he decided to retire - which he never ended up completely doing.

Trooper #216 Wes Benitz
Missouri State Highway Patrol
Unionville, Missouri

"If Doc Judd had not been Doc Judd, he probably would have been Officer Judd, Sheriff Judd, or even Trooper Judd. Doc always wanted to be where the action was. That is testified to by his being a Coroner for over 40 years, or maybe by seeing officers sitting on the square at 2:00 AM and Doc wanting to talk with you until 4 – 5 AM just because he wanted to talk and find out what was going on. Sometimes he might even circle the square half a dozen times and then come down to the Sheriff's Office to find out who we just drug into jail.

Whether I came to Doc's office as a Trooper or as a patient, Doc was always helpful and had time to talk. With a lot of other doctors, that is not always so."

Seth Bruce

Thank You, Dr. Judd

"It would be nice if we could both walk good enough to go to my timber and get a nice mess of young squirrel like we did one time.

Remember the night it was raining and my mules got out on the highway and I couldn't get around them and you came along in your jeep and we run them back home and I went with you down in Sullivan County to see a boy with pneumonia, the jeep done it's stud that night. I also remember the night you took me out of the hay baler. Thank you Dr. Judd".

Clark and Arabelle Carter

Football Doc

"Clark's first memories of Dr. Judd were when he took care of his father, **Oscar Carter**, for many years. Oscar had bone cancer and was bedfast for two years before he died. This was in the early 1950's and Clark was a teenager. Since the family did not have a telephone, Clark would go to the Kozy Korner Service Station and call the Dr. at all times of the night or day. Of course he always came and gave Mr. Carter a shot of morphine or whatever he needed at the time to relieve the pain. Dr. Judd also took care of Clark's mother and other members of the family.

Clark remembers when he was playing football and Doc was always there and when a player got hurt he would run out on the field and be there before the player was hardly aware that he had been hurt.

He has been the master of ceremonies or the featured speaker at many functions in the area but especially at the football banquets.

He always heard, "there goes Dr. Judd' whether he was really going anywhere or not, I don't know, but he made you think he was.

There's a story that everyone knows about the time he was stopped for speeding by the highway patrolman out east of town in the Blackbird bottoms, and when the officer asked to see his pilot's license the good doctor showed them to him and he was sent on his way. As Doc's 'running' out onto the football field slowed to a fast walk, I think his driving has also slowed down. I'm not saying he is slowing down because he's getting older but because he is just wiser.

In 1981 Doc told me I needed to have my gallbladder removed and I was not happy with this diagnosis, so I tried to live with it for nine months. Then one day I called the clinic and said I wanted the thing removed. Doc performed the surgery and I recovered very well and have been happy to have had the surgery."

Irene Comstock

Cleaning Chickens

"Doc, you were always buying things off of your patients to help them out in paying their bills. This time it was capons from **Mrs. Head** in Pollock.

Ruth and I set a date to pick clean them as we were always doing things together (canning, making candy and even cleaning chickens). Work was more fun that way and we always did everything in large quantities and them we would divide.

About noon the day we were to clean the capons, we were in full gear when we heard a car come in the drive and go to the back to park. It was Doc and he had brought a doctor friend from Kirksville home with him for lunch. When he saw the mess we were in he just said, "What in the hell are you girls up to now? And do you really have to use the new station wagon as a chicken coup?" You see when Mrs. Head brought the chickens we set the coup inside the station wagon and we would take out two at a time to clean them but somehow the lid had some undone and the chickens had gotten out in the station wagon. The poor chickens were so scared they were flying all over the car. They were standing on the back of the seats and in fact almost everything was flying around in there!"

John and Etta Comstock

Our Trip West

"Back in 1945 we were privileged to go on a trip with Doc and Ruth and this took us to varied places in Colorado and other points west. What a fun trip this was. We left in the middle of the night from Unionville, drove all night and the 1946 V8 Ford got us to Colorado by noon the next day. Of course we would get lost daily as we started out to venture toward a different mountain and sight each day. We drove all day, turned in early, ate a good evening meal and then started all over the next day to explore something big and spectacular. Doc would get up very early each morning, go out to the motel parking lot or coffee shop and get acquainted with the natives. He would invariable end up with a patient or two.

From Colorado we traveled to Salt Lake City, Utah. There we heard the Mormon Tabernacle Choir on Sunday morning. We left a piece of our luggage in Salt Lake City, so we had to call back and have that sent to us by plane to Pocatello, Idaho. The plane landed in a cow pasture there.

One time when seasonal colds were prevalent, I was hospitalized with respiratory problems. When the nurse took me to my room, lo and behold, there was my sister in the other bed as my roommate. Dr. Judd had entered her the same day with practically the same thing, and slyly hadn't told either of us, because he had arranged this 'getting together' as a surprise, which was so typical of him. Unpredictable!!! But we all had a good time in spite of the pills, etc.

Rex Cooley

High School Friends

Charles and I attended high school together in Powersville, Mo when James and his wife, Mary, taught there. Charles had it rough because he never got a break under them.

Both of us belonged to the Lion's Club in Unionville for many years. Doc always made a great effort to attend and was very dedicated to the principles of the club. The thing I remember about Doc most was the many stories he told every day. It seemed he always had a new one and I enjoyed every one of them.

Fay Galloway

The Confinement Case

"As I have said many times, Dr. Judd went regardless of the weather or conditions. When sickness called he was there through rain, sleet, snow, hail, mud roads or tornadoes. I know for he has doctored three generations of our family.

The night following my husband, Neal's funeral, the doctor came by and told us that the funeral had touched him as nothing had since his father and mother had passed away. The feeling was mutual too, for Neal wished almost every day that Dr. Judd could come by and visit with him. He almost always told him a little joke or something about Pollock. It reminds me of one of his first confinement cases. The family lived near Pollock and they had never come to see the Doc until the husband came to get him that night. After a short while, one baby came and the doctor told him he's have to take the one baby as he was sure there was another one coming. Just as the man sat down on the trunk at the foot of the bed with the baby, the woman gave one of the most ungodly yells he had every heard and an old dog that was under the bed grabbed Doc's ankle. It scared him so badly that he almost dropped the baby, and he never knew who have that awful yell, he or the woman. As all this excitement was taking place, the husband fainted."

Leonard and Georgia Hamilton

Our Three Babies

Our family started doctoring with Dr. Judd in the fall of 1942 when he had his practice in Pollock. We had three children and Dr. Judd delivered all three.

The first was born April 26, 1943 in a rainstorm. We lived three miles southeast of Boynton on a dirt road. A tree fell across the road and John Vaughn, the closest neighbor, had to pull Doc's car up the hill with a team of horses so he could bring **Robert** into the world.

Jerry just about didn't wait for Doc to come help him arrive on Flag Day, June 14, 1947. The following day was Father's Day and Georgia took castor oil and forgot to ask Doc how long to wait before coming to the hospital!

Judy came in a blizzard on March 5, 1953. Leonard took Georgia up to the old Monroe Hospital and left her there with friends to wait. He then went to push snow to get **June Wagoner** out of her road to have her baby. A friend came by to tell him that he had a girl this time.

We have enjoyed having Doc for a friend and doctor for over 42 years. No matter what time of day or night he was always there to help.

Betty Head

Friend Faithful

I tried to think of the first time I met Dr. Judd but I was so young, about six, that I don't really remember except I look at it like a piece of cloth and you can't find that first thread that starts the cloth. I just remember going to him for treatments from the time I was very young. I do remember his mustache and how I wondered how he kept it looking so nice and neat. It was interesting to me because no one else I knew had a mustache. Then there were the times he was setting on the porch in front of his office as I came by on my way home from school. He always had time to visit.

Of course everyone remembers the night **William** was born. I got up to see what all the noise was about but was soon told to go back to bed. It was too cold to stand there in bare feet and argue so I went to bed. When we got up in the morning there was a new baby. I think Willie was the first of ours you delivered but by no means the last. Out of 32 grandchildren for my parents you delivered 21 and it didn't stop there. Out of 16 great grandchildren you delivered five and you even delivered one of the two great-great grandchildren.

You were always there for me. You wiped my tears when I was in pain, gave me sympathy when I needed it and laughed with me many times."

Nina Hines

Memories of a Nurse and Friend

I have asked around the hospital trying to have others help me remember things of interest to share but truthfully, Dr. Judd's memory is much better than ours.

Virginia Bruckshaw is still wondering what went on at one of the Lion's Club cookouts where Dr. Judd frequently bar-b-qued. Her husband, Jim, was supposed to be helping one night but he came home dead drunk!

An elderly lady in the office one day says, "Dr. Judd, my husband is a homosexual. Without batting an eye Doc said, "Oh, he is?" And the lady replied, 'yes, Ralph is a homosexual. He just wants sex at home all the time!"

I also remember one lady who called wanting Doc to make a house call because the weather was too bad for her to get out and come to the office. And he went!

Another incident that amused me greatly was the man that came in Doc's office and after he was examined Doc told him he had gonorrhea. Trying to find out where he got it so that person could be treated also, Doc carefully questioned the man. Finally the man said, "Oh, hell! I don't know if I got it from my wife or my girlfriend, they're both running around on me!"

About 8 am at the hospital in Unionville, the phone rang. The lady's request was for Dr. Judd to come to Powersville because her husband had fallen on the ice. She said, "I think he has broken his hip but I want you to check him out and be sure it's broken before I call the ambulance to take him to Centerville to the hospital" I don't think he answered that call.

Soon after the ambulance service was taken from the funeral homes by the county, we got an ambulance call that **Roy Robbins** had been hit by a high voltage wire. **Jim Bruckshaw** was a member of the ambulance crew at the time so away he and Doc flew to answer the call, not knowing how bad the electric shock had been. Anxiously, I waited at the base radio for word. Finally, Dr. Judd was on the radio giving me a report. "Well, our patient is alert and conscious but has some burns so we are bring him in. We were delayed here for a while with Jim. He tripped over a tom cat's tail and the cat scratched his leg and I had to take some time to fix that up." Knowing Doc's ability to make up stories, I didn't believe it until they got back with Jim's leg for proof.

Everyone knows Dr. Judd's love of a good joke, either telling or listening, but few knew or saw the quiet, silent grieving side that I have seen from a very caring doctor who lost a young patient. It was often the same with many coroner's cases for him, because these were not just patients, they were friends and neighbors that he had known for many years.

I have worked with Dr. Judd since April 15, 1964. During that time we have had up to 50 patients a day go through the office. We've had several doctors come and go. Remember Dr. **Gray, Dr. Herren, Dr. Nuhn**, **Dr. Anderson**, **Dr. Brackett**, **Dr. Drake**, **Dr. McDonald, Dr. Casady** and **Dr. O'Brien.** Today (2003) **Dr. Casady**, **Dr. Abid**, and **Dr. Williams** are still in Unionville along with Dr. Judd.

According to the OR record logbook at Putnam County Memorial Hospital, Dr. Judd had performed or assisted with 2,037 surgeries there between 1963 and 1984. He also administered anesthetics for many others. The OB record shows he has delivered 1020 babies at this hospital. I know he delivered a lot more (over 3,500) but remember I'm talking just since PCMH opened on Oct. 13, 1963.

Oh, yes, I'm sure no one, especially Dr. Judd, will forget the hobo from the train wreck that never regained consciousness. He lived in the hospital from July until the following January before he died.

Chapter 32

My Doctor, My Friend, My Husband
by
Carolyn Smart Bomgardner Judd

My parents, Dean and Helen Smart lived about one mile from Plainview Cemetery in Sullivan County, Missouri. They lived on the farm that was homesteaded by my Grandfather, H.K. Smart. It was about five miles (going west) to the Judd farm.

Mother always had her nieces, **Virginia Melton (Gibson)** and **Mary Jo Melton (McCellen)** come to the farm and visit during the summer. In the late 1930's Mary Jo and Virginia were washing their hair in the back room from the kitchen. They were done and went to open the back door to throw the water out and about that time Jim and Charles Judd, who brought ice for the 'ice box' were coming in to replenish the ice and the girls threw the water on them and then screamed. Because they had no blouses on the girls, as well as the boys, were scared beyond talking. Jim and Charles had an ice route in the area and Charles said they went to Trenton to get the ice.

My brothers, **Raynor** and **Russell Smart** and I were born in Centerville, Iowa, but soon after that, Dr. Judd came to Pollock so he became our only doctor. I remember how mad I was at Dr. Judd one time when the folks called him to come to the farmhouse and I was in bed with a fever and so sick. He just walked in the back door and told mother I had the measles. He could smell them as he had a very keen sense of smell for many diseases. I was mad because I wanted the doctor to look at me and give me some attention.

When I was about eight or nine years old I had an attack of appendicitis and my parents took me to the doctor's office in Pollock. Dr. Judd didn't want me to go back home so I went up to his house. I stayed the whole day with Ruth, and I remember that she had a beautiful cut glass candy dish sitting on the table filled with candy. She let me have some when I got to feeling better. That evening, the folks came to pick me up. When I was thirteen years old I did have to have my appendix taken out. Dr. Judd did it one night and I got along just fine and was soon back in school.

Dad had a heart attack in the late 1940's and Dr. Judd would come to the farm everyday and take care of Dad's medical needs. He spent many hours, day and night, caring for Dad. One night we didn't think Dad would live. I was crying and Dr. Judd came and sat by me and explained what was happening and how I had to be strong to help Mother. He always had the words and kind touch of comfort.

Sometimes when Dr. Judd came to the farm, Serece would come with him, and play with me, and the boys. We just loved to have her come with him. Dr. Judd would load a large EKG machine and haul it to the farm in the back of his jeep. Dad made it through all of this illness and lived several more years.

Dr. Judd was my doctor and delivered my four children, **David, Joan, Glenda** and **Tom Bomgardner.** He took care of our family and the kids through all their illnesses.

My husband, **Don Bomgardner** and I, lived in Arizona during the 1980's and when my mother became ill in 1989 I came back to take care of her. In 1990 we moved to Kansas City to be near Raynor and Russell, where it would be easier for them to help me care for Mother. In 1994 mother required more help than we could give and she wanted to go to the Milan Care Center. Her granddaughter, Marti Smart Jones, was the nursing Director there. After only a few weeks, mother died. This was during the holidays and Christmas time so Dr. Judd wasn't at Mother's visitation or funeral. He had already gone to Lee's Summit to visit his daughter and family. Mother's sister, Aunt Ruth Pollock, died in October the next year. Dr. Judd was at her visitation and we talked then and did a lot of catching up. By then I was divorced from Don and living in Kansas City. I told Dr. Judd to call when he was down at Serece's during the holidays. When he was down for Thanksgiving he did call and we went out to eat that evening. We had a nice dinner and I was smiling and thinking, "Never in my dreams did I think I would be having a date and dinner with my doctor and good friend all of my life, but there I was".

We talked on the phone several times and saw each other again during the Christmas holidays. In the early spring I was going to Arizona to visit friends and Dr. Judd wanted to go too and see his sister who lived in Sun City. On the plane, on the way home, Dr. Judd asked me if I would marry him and move to Unionville. I couldn't believe he really meant me and I even asked, "Do you mean me?"

November 14, 1997 we were married and on the following Sunday morning we went to church in Unionville. What a shock the people had, seeing us together. The heads really turned and the whispers were going wild. We got many chuckles through the years about that morning.

My kids, family, and friends enjoyed having us come to their homes and getting to know Dr. Judd as a person instead of only their doctor. Everyone loved to hear about his cars and interesting house calls.

We spent many nights with Serece and Ron and their family too. When I had back surgery we were at their home for several weeks as I recovered.

Our years together were the most wonderful years of my life. Dr. Judd was my doctor, my best friend, and then my husband. I just give praise and thank God for allowing me and our family to have the strength to take care of him at Serece's home during his final days.

Dad and Carolyn in 1998

Chapter 33
Masons

Dad started his Masonic membership on Oct. 8, 1938 as a Fellowcraft and became a full member of the Putnam Lodge #190 in Newtown, Missouri on November 5, 1938.

On April 15, 1941 he transferred his membership to the Pollock Lodge and received his 50-year pin there in December of 1988.

On Sept 16, 1997 he became a duel member after joining the Hartford Lodge #171.

Freemasonry dates back hundreds of years to when stonemasons and other craftsmen worked together. Shriners belong to the Ancient Arabic Order of the Mystic Shrine for North America. Shrine is an international fraternity and a man must adhere to the principles of Freemasonry to become a Shriner. They have an emphasis on philanthropy as evidenced by the Shriner's Children's Hospitals around the country. Most people think of them as clowns in parades, the guys with the funny cars and motorcycles in parades, and the men with the funny hats that stand out in front of stores as they sell tickets to the

Shriner's Circus. All these activities, along with many others, are an effort to raise money for the children.

One thing Dad was good at and enjoyed was memorization and he could recite the entire Masonic ritual at funerals for his fallen brothers. His good friend and fellow Mason, **Melvin Hall** said he had given 99 Masonic funeral services and that Dad assisted him in 46 of them. Dad's first Masonic funeral was given on July 16, 1990 and his last was May 16, 2002. He would always end the funeral service by reciting the poem "Crossing the Bar**".   Donald Noland** is now using that poem to end the services.

Crossing the Bar
Alfred Lord Tennyson

Sunset and evening star,
And one clear call for me,
And may there be no moaning of the bar,
When I put out to sea.
But such a tide as moving seems asleep,
Too full for sound and foam,
When that which drew from out the boundless deep
Turns again home.
Twilight and evening bell
And after that the dark!
And may there be no sadness of farewell,
When I embark;
For tho'from out our bourne of time and place
The flood may bear me far,
I hope to see my Pilot face to face
When I have crossed the bar.

Dad and Melvin went to the Grand Lodge of Missouri meetings three different years. Melvin said Dad filled in any office that was needed and that he liked to help others become members. He served as Chaplin at least 10 years in Pollock.

Melvin expressed how much he really misses the old Doc, and even had the thought go through his head not long ago to call him when his wife was feeling poorly.

Another fellow Mason was **Donovan Poland**. Although Dad didn't attend much until he was mostly retired, from 1990 on he rarely missed a meeting. Donovan or Melvin and Dad would car pool to Pollock and Hartford to the meetings. In Pollock, the meeting room was up some steep stairs above the bank building and when Dad was not able to climb the stairs because of chest pains, they moved the meeting to the lower level. Donovan would go to Pollock with Dad every week and stopped by his office regularly to give him the Milan or Des Moines papers.

As I was visiting with Melvin he told me about the time he cut his head when a pony cart went through a gate and tossed him out. The nurse thought Dad was taking a long time with the stitching, which wasn't necessary because the cut was way up above the hairline. Dad wanted to make it as neat as possible and it's a good thing he did because today Melvin is bald. One night a group of friends were traveling to Canton, Missouri to a music show and some were teasing Melvin about being bald. Because Dad was along, Melvin said it was his fault he was bald because when he took his appendix out in 1945 he wrapped an elastic bandage so tight it pushed him right up through his hair.

Melvin had many experiences with his good doctor starting in 1944 when he was three years old. Melvin cut his thumb off. Dad sewed it back on and for several weeks there was no feeling in it, but finally life returned, and today it is quite functional.

Chapter 34

Dr. Judd nominated for Country Doctor of the Year

By Nina Rexroat

This article appeared in the Unionville Republican on January 10, 1996. Nina Rexroat, a longtime friend, and nurse at the Putnam County Hospital, nominated Dr. C.L. Judd for Country Doctor of the Year in 1994. Although Staff Care, Inc., sponsor of the award, selected Dr. William Hill of Carrollton, Alabama as the national winner, Dr. Judd will still be the winner in the hearts of many Putnam County residents.

The following is the cover letter written by Nina Rexroat that was submitted with the application.

The icon of old country doctors in my opinion is Dr. Charles L. Judd who has been in family practice in the Unionville, MO area since 1940. Even now, at the age of 78, he still has an office in his home where he sees several patients per day.

He was born on a farm near Newtown, MO, 20 miles southwest of Unionville on December 23, 1916. His schooling was eight years in a one-room country school near his home, high school in Newtown and graduation from Powersville, MO. Then he went on to Kirksville, MO for college and medical school. He graduated from the Kirksville College of Osteopathic Medicine in 1940.

His first practice was started in Pollock, MO (11 miles south of Unionville) in June 1940. In 1944, he moved his practice to Unionville where he still remains.

His scope of practice covered six decades of service to his fellowman and included much more than just a busy medical practice. He was county corner for over 40 years. He has been a Masonic Member 57 years (he received his 60 year pin in 1998) and a member of the Order of Eastern Star as long. Many years of service has also been given as an active member of Lions Club, Shriners, Putnam County Health Department Board, Putnam County Ambulance Board, Putnam County Nutrition Board, and the Missouri State Crippled Children's Advisory Board. He was Unionville's Citizen of the month, a Distinguished Patron for Kirksville College of Osteopathic Medicine as well as receiving the Diplomatic Award. He also spent many hours of work getting the new county hospital built when the state rules forced him and his partner to close their private hospital. He is an active member of the First Christian Church of Unionville.

The county school system will long remember his many hours devoted to the sports department. Every year as school began he was there doing free sports physicals. Every game, if an emergency didn't prevent, would find Dr. Judd there to support the Putnam County Midgets. If there was an injury he was there to help before the player hardly knew he was injured. He served without charge as their doctor for 40 plus years.

Over the years, he has delivered over 3,500 babies. For many that he delivered in the early 1940's, he went on to deliver the second and third generations in the families. One lady who refused to allow anyone else to deliver her baby started labor while Dr. Judd was with his family vacationing in Minnesota. He was notified and drove 10 hours home in time to deliver her child before heading back to his family in Minnesota.

Dr. Judd was always in the hospital by 7 am to make morning rounds for 20 to 30 patients. Then it was off to the clinic where he has seen as many as 100 patients in one day. The door of the clinic was never locked until the last patient had been seen. Then it was home to eat supper with his wife and daughter, if time would permit, and then back to the hospital for evening rounds and house calls. He continued to make house calls long after most doctors had stopped. In fact he will still make a house call today!

This doctor's practice has gone from mud roads to pavements, horse and buggies to jeeps and streamlined cars, home deliveries under a shade tree on a hot summer day to modern birthing rooms, doing all his own general surgeries to specialists of all kinds, sulfa drugs to a wide range of antibiotics, and payment of bills with chickens and produce to Medicare and Medicaid.

Probably the most stressful week of his entire career began May 22, 1962 when a Boeing 707 jet crashed a few miles north of Unionville, killing all 45 passengers on board. As coroner, Dr. Judd, worked practically around the clock for the next four days. Now, 33 years later, the memories that stand out are not the long hours and hard work, but the personal letters of praise for a job well done that he received from the President of Continental Airlines, Missouri State Attorney General, Head of the Federal Aviation Agency, and even the Director of the FBI, J. Edgar Hoover.

Services were always given because of Doc's dedication to helping others – not for the monetary gain. Over the years, I have many times heard him say 'just mark that off the bill. They can't afford to pay anyway'. Never once do I remember hearing him ask a patient how he planned to pay a bill. Many times he already knew he would never be paid. His only concern was that the patient was sick and needed help, so he treated them.

Although his medical skills are legendary in Putnam County, his storytelling was also well known. People began to suggest he write a book about his experiences. As a result, in July 1990 *Reminiscences of a Country Doctor* as told to his daughter, Serece, was printed as a soft cover book.

In 1984, Dr. Judd decided to retire. Two weeks later our beloved doctor suffered a heart attack. That was later followed with a four by-pass heart surgery. Following his recovery, he was ready to leave retirement and return to the practice he loved so well. Recently, visiting with his daughter, Serece, she said, "Today is Saturday but Dad saw 12 patients".

Dr. Judd is now in his fifty-fifth year of practice. He walks two miles a day and his mind remains extremely sharp. It has certainly been a privilege to know him. Most of us emulate this man and wish we could be the same type of individual.

Thank you for considering Dr. Charles L. Judd for Country Doctor of the Year, as I feel he is truly deserving of the honor.

Chapter 35
A Tribute to Dr. Judd
By
Nancy Mullenix

One day while visiting my uncle's grave in the west end of the Unionville Cemetery, I was looking at new stones that had been set. I happened upon one who I feel I have known very well over the years of my life. It seemed to me to be too modest for someone who has given so much to our community. It was a pretty mahogany stone but held only his name, date, Masonic, Order of Eastern Star and Shriners emblems.

The first encounters I had with his kind was what seemed to me to be a very old gentleman who our family had trusted many times with our lives. His office was in Green City and I can still recall the medicinal smells of his office that was located in his home. He had treated my grandmother for many years for a heart condition and it was commonly thought there could be no other who could properly manage her medical care. One day, however, we received word of the death of the kind doctor. The time was somewhere in the late 1940's.

We had heard good reports from a young doctor in Unionville by the name of Charles L. Judd. It was decided after hearing he was good at treating heart problems, he would be a good doctor for my dear grandmother. From that time forward he would be our family doctor and we found him to be just as we had heard. The next time I would see him myself was in June of 1950 when he would deliver my beautiful baby brother, Tom David. I can still see the doctor who had assisted my mother, who was thought to be to old to bear a child! This Dr. Charles L. Judd was dressed to the hilt with a light colored double-breasted suit, white shirt, wide tie and black and white spectator shoes of the highest fashion. I remember also the car he drove which was very flashy and it was always ready to rush to any emergency or to make any house calls. As a child, I was very impressed with this great doctor.

The next time I would see him was when he treated me for severe throat problems. Finally he told my parents it was his opinion an operation for removal of my tonsils was necessary to solve my problems. In no time at all I was brought to the old Monroe Hospital where I had met my brother for the first time.

It was also the same place where my dear grandmother had spent her last days and my cousin and I had been there with our families playing on the lawn and sitting in the large lobby with the glassed in stairway going up to the hospital rooms.

It was in the days of ether and I was whisked away early one morning to a large operating room with bright lights. It was a strange scary place for a small girl with long pigtails and very large eyes I am sure!

Shortly after entering the room the kind Dr. Judd came to my side and his kind, gentle touch soothed my fears. I can recall the odor of the ether that was in the mask and was placed on my face. I was asked to count to ten, but before I reached that number, I saw a bright array of stairs. The next thing I remember was being in an upstairs ward room with the most terrible sore throat I had ever experienced! My faithful doctor, however, was present to give his support to my parents and me.

There are other things also I recall over the years about this hometown doctor, such as the jeep he drove through mud roads to reach the people who were dear to his heart. There was never a storm or circumstance too great for him to tackle to reach those who needed him.

With all these thoughts and many more in mind, I approached our Dr. Judd and asked him if I could write a tribute for an inscription on a footstone that I believed was needed.

He reluctantly said it was fine. I thought it should be in place for him to see because I believe in giving roses while we can still smell and enjoy them.

I compiled a long page which was of course, impossible to place on a footstone but **Merle Lewis** took the page and condensed it into the footstone one can see today.

I know I am not alone in my feeling toward this doctor who has had a great dedication to his profession and has given so much of himself to our community and the surrounding area.

The footstone inscription on the grave of Dr. C.L. Judd in the Unionville Cemetery reads as follows:

" He never refused the calls of the sick and the dying. Whether wealthy or poor his compassion and humor eased the hard times and we are the better for his having been here. Friends"

Chapter 36
Dad's Cars

Since 1938 Dad must have had about 60 new cars. He usually kept two at a time – one for a family car and one for use in his practice because until 1980 he made a lot of house calls all over the country. He would go as far as 35 miles to make a house call and he put many miles on his car going back and forth to the hospital in Unionville. He put more miles on by going to the hospital in Kirksville, MO also.

Dad owned everything from Model A's to Lincolns and Cadillacs, along with jeeps and Corvettes. (find the full list at the end of this chapter) He couldn't help taking the challenge from other drivers when it came to deciding whose car could run the fastest. In 1957 and 1959 he owned Corvettes – a red and white '57 and a metallic blue '59. These cars were so much faster in the 50's than they are today because they didn't have all the gadgets on them to slow them down and there weren't many speed limits either. No one ever passed Dad, if he didn't want them to do so. One time he bet a gentleman, who owned a little cub airplane, $5 that he could beat him from the airport to Hartford, which was nine miles of straight road. Dad knew the plane could only go 80 to 90 miles per hour and his Corvette could travel at 100 miles per hour easily. There were no curves that would slow him down, so he was confident of winning the bet. The airplane took off from the airport and when he reached the side of the road, Dad took off, and he reached Hartford at least two, maybe three minutes before the airplane arrived. On the stretch of road at the creek bottom, Dad opened the thing up to 120 miles per hour, and with the top down he could glance up once in awhile to make sure he was well ahead of the plane. Now, these speeds were something he didn't want his daughter to know anything about.

One day when Dad was at the hospital working, a call came in from about twelve miles out in the country. It was on a very crooked blacktop road that a fellow had had a heart attack out in the field. They wanted the doctor to come quickly. Dad took off down the road and as he neared the edge of town he saw a patrol car. This particular patrolman had a Dodge patrol car and he had made brags that no one could get away from him. When Dad saw him he thought to himself, "I don't have time to fool with him, I've got to take care of a sick man." So he wound 'er up tight and turned off the main highway onto the crooked blacktop road. The Corvette could take the curves much better than the Dodge and so Dad was doing one mile for every half mile the patrolman made. The patrolman went back up to the hospital and asked a nurse, "Was Doc Judd in a hurry when he left town awhile ago? He'd better have been!" The nurse said, "Yes, a man had a heart attack southeast of town and they told Doc to come quickly. You know Doc, he's going to go quickly!" The patrolman wanted to make sure, or otherwise he was going to arrest the doctor.

Dad owned Chevrolets, Pontiacs, Chryslers, Oldsmobiles, Cadillacs, Lincolns, and Fords; you name it, and he probably owned one. Besides these cars, he wore out three jeeps. I got to drive the jeeps to school because he didn't usually use them during the daytime. I had more fun with the jeep than I ever could have had with a new car. **Sharon Herrick** and I even took off one day and drove it to Newtown (more than 30 miles away) to see Grandma Judd. This was just shortly after I got my drivers license. Many times I loaded that jeep full of girls and hauled them all over the place.

Even though Dad drove hundreds of thousands of miles in his automobiles, he was lucky not to have had too many accidents. One wreck happened just west of Lucerne and it involved a cow. The farmer was moving the cow from one pasture to another one across the highway when Dad topped the hill. The car surprised the farmer so much that he turned the cow around and that put her right in the car's path. Dad spent several days in the hospital over that one and the bones that weren't broken felt like they were. But even at his worst, Dad was better off than the cow that failed to survive.

During a snowstorm in the winter of 1950, Dad had another accident. A lady from Livonia had just started home with her young son, who was just big enough to stand in the floorboard and look through the windshield. When she came to the curve down by the Country Club, she saw the other car and became a little excited. She slammed on the brakes and started skidding across the road toward Dad. He tried to dodge her by going toward the ditch, but he couldn't get out of her way, and they practically hit head on. Fortunately, no one was hurt, but the little boy was quoted as saying, "Oh goody, goody, Mother, it's Doctor Judd! We hit him!"

The worst wreck that he ever had was in the winter of 1952. It was suspected that **Jeanette Worley** had polio and Dad was taking her, along with her mother, to the hospital in Kirksville. The accident happened about two miles south of the junction of Highways 63 and 136 at Lancaster, Missouri. According to the police report, the Judd car was going south and the other car, driven by Marvin Moffitt of Bloomfield, Iowa, was headed north. The latter car was noted to be weaving from side to side as it approached, and then suddenly attempted to make a U turn on the highway ahead of the approaching Judd car, which was too close to stop. Both cars were badly damaged and one man, Benny Ritz, of Troy, Iowa, was killed. Several other people in the Ritz automobile were injured. Dad had three broken ribs and lacerations on his legs and face. Mrs. Worley suffered a broken right wrist and hand and several lacerations on her face and head. Jeanette had a deep cut on her right leg.

Because Mom owned a flower shop and had to haul a lot of fresh flowers, a big, heavy, Oldsmobile station wagon was the family car in 1959. Dad didn't own a jeep that winter and so he hired **John Carman** to go with him on country calls when there was a big snow. That way

John could help him shovel out of the drifts so they could make it to the patient's home.

The winter of 1959 proved to be a real challenge, since there was many snow storms that year. I remember several weeks in a row when it would start snowing on Wednesday afternoon and we wouldn't have school Thursday or Friday. I remember we had to make up those missed days by attending a Saturday or two and extending the school day by an hour each day.

One particular night that winter, Dad was called to Pollock and he got John Carman to accompany him. Between Lemon and Pollock there were stretches of clear road between huge drifts that were building up fast. Dad spotted a big drift ahead, and he figured if he went fast enough on the bare spot before the drift, that big Oldsmobile could plow right through. Dad warned John, "Hang on John, we're going to have to hit this one hard to make it through!" They plowed into the drift and when the car came to a stop the snow was up over the radiator, and up to the doors. They had to roll the windows down and scoop snow away in order to get the doors open and get out of the drift. About one-half mile farther down the road Dad could see another drift. John hollered this time, "Hold it! Stop this damn thing right now! If you're going to hit this drift like the last one I want to walk." To this Dad explained, "John, this snow is soft, hitting it won't hurt us. John's answer, "Maybe not, but there might be somebody as crazy as you coming through from the other direction!" Dad made it through that drift and John had to walk about a half mile down the road to catch up with the station wagon again.

The last wreck that I can remember Dad having was one winter in the early 1990's. He was on his way to Unionville from our home in Lee's Summit in a snowstorm. When he wrecked the air bags deployed and that was a new, big surprise for him. Air bags and seat belts were unheard of when he did his 'fast' driving.

Cars Owned by Dad Through the Years

Ford

1929 **Model A (bought in 1939)**
1930 **Model A (bought in 1940)**
1941 **2 door Deluxe**
1942 **2 door Deluxe**
1946 **4 passenger coupe**

Chevrolet

1947 **Station Wagon**
1951 **4 door**
1953 **4 door**
1955 **2 door hardtop**
1957 **Station Wagon**
1958 **Station Wagon**
1957 **red Corvette**
1958 **silver Corvette**

Oldsmobile

1949 **Station Wagon**
1951 **4 door sedan**
1953 **"88" hard top (wrecked)**
1957 **4 door hard top**
1958 **4 door hard top**
1961 **Starfire convertible**
1985 **Toronado**

Buick

1957
1963
1965
1967
1969 Station Wagon
1971
1982

Jeep

1946 jeepster
1946
1948
1952
1956
1961 hard top

Lincoln

1972 Mark II
1974 Mark IV
1977 Mark IV
1979 Mark V

Pontiac

1947 4 door sedan
1949 4 door sedan

Dodge

1952

Chrysler

1948 Town & Country
1948 4 door sedan (wrecked)

Cadillac

1949 wrecked (hit a cow)
1951 2 door (wrecked)
1952 2 door
1953 2 door
1954 2 door
1955 2 door
1956 2 door
1957 2 door
1958 2 door

1990 4 door
1993 4 door
1994 4 door
1998 4 door
1999 4 door
2002 4 door (wrecked)
2004 4 door

1931 Ford Model A

1958 Chevrolet Corvette

2004 Cadillac DeVille

Chapter 37
Some Advances in Medicine from 1916 to 2004

1921

-The Band-Aid brand adhesive bandages hit the market.

1921

-Insulin was used for the treatment of diabetes. Two Canadians, Frederick Banting (1891 – 1941) and Charles Best (1800 – 1978) saved a dying diabetic patient with this experimental drug.

1924

-The Electroencephalogram (EEG). Hans Berger (1873 – 1941) a German psychiatrist expanded on Wilhelm Einthvon's work with Electrocardiograms (ECG).

1928

-Penicillin is discovered. Alexander Fleming (1881 – 1955) a Scottish physician found a blue mold that killed bacteria.

1932

-Dr. L.W. McDonald begins medical practice in Powersville, MO.

1937

-First blood bank. Bernard Fantus set this up at Cook County Hospital in Chicago.

1940

-Dr. C.L. Judd begins his medical practice in Pollock, MO.

1943

-Discovery of streptomycin to cure tuberculosis and meningitis. Selman Waksman (1888 – 1973) Russian born American microbiologist.

1944

-First open-heart surgery. Alfred Blalock (1899 – 1964) successfully developed a shunt to bypass an obstruction in the aorta of a 15-month old baby girl.

1945

-First kidney dialysis machine.

1948

-Cortisone used to treat rheumatoid arthritis (Philip Hench (1896 - 1965).

1950

-First successful organ transplant, a kidney, by Richard Lawler and James West.

1953

 -James Watson, Francis Crick, Rosalind Franklin and Maurice Wilkins

 discovered the structure of DNA.

1954

-Jonas Salk develops polio vaccine. Nationwide immunizations first given in 1955.

1960

-Birth control pill approved for general use in United States.

First pacemaker inserted.

1962

-David Sabiston performs first coronary bypass at Johns Hopkins.

1965

-President Lyndon Johnson enacts Medicare and Medicaid legislation.

1967

-Christian Barnard performs first heart transplant (South Africa).

1978

-Louise Brown is first test-tube baby.

1980

-Smallpox eradicated worldwide.

1981

-MRI (Magnetic resonance imaging) first used.

1983

-AIDS virus identified.

1996

-Dolly (cloned sheep) born in Scotland.

This list could be much longer and the last 10 years have shown many, many more life saving discoveries. The 20th century has seen the most rapid development in medicine. During the 19th century the life expectancy rose from 40 to 50 years, but in the 20th century it increased to nearly 80 years.

A survey was taken in 2000 at a conference of Infectious Disease Physicians in Dallas, TX. They were asked to name the top 10 infectious disease events of the past century (in rank order). They came up with the following results:

1. Eradication of smallpox
2. Discovery of penicillin
3. Epidemic of HIV
4. Epidemic of influenza 1918 – 19
5. Polio vaccine
6. Childhood immunization
7. Antibiotic resistance
8. Tuberculosis
9. Cultivation of infectious agents
10. Chlorination of water

Chapter 38
What is Osteopathy?

The citizens of Northeast Missouri have no question about what Osteopathy is because there are more Osteopaths in the communities around Kirksville than any other kind of doctor.

Dr. Andrew Taylor Still was the founder of the school. The first class graduated in 1894 with 21 members, including five women and four of Dr. Still's children.

As a young boy, Andrew liked to go with his father, a doctor, on house calls as he tended to broken bones and stopped the flow of blood in his patients. He also liked to hunt and while skinning the animals he had killed, he studied the bones, muscles and nerves, seeing how they all seemed to be associated in the animals. His early schooling was in Tennessee ,but then he continued somewhat sporadically in log cabin schools in Missouri. Finally, he attended a school in LaPlata, Missouri run by the Cumberland Presbyterian Church.

Dr. Andrew Still's medical education, typical of that day, was acquired by being an apprentice with his father as the tutor. After he married at age 21, the family moved to Kansas. In Kansas he was active in the border warfare and served as a scout-surgeon to General John C. Fremont, and at age 29 was elected to the Kansas State legislature. His first wife died leaving him with three small children, and then he married Mary E. Turner. In the early 1860's he attended the College of Physicians and Surgeons in Kansas City.

He served in the Union Army during the Civil War as a surgeon. During the war, he became concerned about the large number of camp deaths and he questioned the present methods of medical treatment. The death rates were extremely high on the battlefront as heavy doses of toxic drugs were given and surgeries were performed in unsanitary conditions without anesthesia. Later, an epidemic of spinal meningitis raged across the Kansas prairie and Dr. Still watched helplessly as three of his own children died from the disease. He decided to devote himself to finding a better method of medicine. For the next 10 years he diligently studied the bones and their relationship to one another, and then the muscles, nerves, and blood. He began to realize that all parts of the body are interrelated, and if one part is diseased it could affect other parts of the body. He discovered how important good circulation was and that the central nervous system was an important system to the whole body. He found that the body contains all the elements necessary for the body to heal itself and a physician, by manipulation, could aid the body in preventing and even curing disease. He called his new theory of medicine "Osteopathy" after the Greek word meaning bone, for he said all his studies started with the bones.

Because of his study, and the philosophy that he had about circulation and healing, many people in Unionville, were spared the severe crippling from Polio that many in other parts of the world were experiencing. As you will read in Chapter 18 on Polio, those of us who got the infectious disease in the early 1950's were given special treatments with hot towels and manipulation several times each day, along with high doses of Vitamin C which was a boost to the immune system.

When Dr. Still attempted to explain osteopathy in Kansas, he was ostracized and called a 'quack' because his method was different from the accepted medical treatment of that day. He decided to return to Missouri, where he had lived for so long, and in 1875 he returned to Kirksville with very little money but lots of determination. He was able to set up his medical practice with the help of several kind supporters in Kirksville. In addition to his growing practice there, Dr. Still became an itinerant doctor, traveling around the state explaining his theory and treating patients. He was helping many people who had not been helped by orthodox medicine. His practice grew so much that he didn't have time to see all his patients, so he decided to start a school and teach his theory to other doctors. He built a small building to house his school and in 1892 opened the American School of Osteopathy. Also the state declared that his graduates could be presented with an M.D. degree, but he chose instead the D.O. for Doctor of Osteopathy.

After he became well known, there were several cities that offered him money and land to move his school to their city. These included Hannibal and Kansas City in Missouri, and Des Moines, Iowa. But Still chose to remain in Kirksville, where everyone had been so kind and helpful to him.

The faculty included Dr. Still, who taught his osteopathic theory and technique, and Dr. William Smith, a graduate of the University of Edinburgh in Scotland, who taught anatomy and other basic sciences. The tuition in 1900 was $500 for the two-year course. Students soon came from all over the United States.

Lame and crippled patients arrived in Kirksville by the hundreds, and the community of Kirksville helped Dr. Still raise money to build a hospital. In 1905 the ASO Hospital was constructed at the corner of Osteopathy and Jefferson Streets. Several hotels and boarding houses were also erected to handle the large number of people arriving there for health care.

New schools began to spring up as osteopathy continued to grow and attract attention in the newspapers and magazines of the country. Even George Bernard Shaw, Mark Twain, and Teddy Roosevelt became advocates of osteopathy. Schools were established in Chicago, Des Moines, Kansas City, Los Angeles and Philadelphia as well as Kirksville. After Dr. Andrew Still died in 1917, his nephew Dr. George Still, became the new president of the ASO. In 1922, Dr. George Laughlin, a son-in-law of A.T. Still, constructed a large brick building at the corner of Jefferson and Elson Streets and opened the Andrew Taylor Still College of Osteopathy and Surgery. In 1925 the two colleges in

Kirksville merged and formed the Kirksville College of Osteopathic Medicine or KCOM as it is often called.

The college course of study expanded to four years and entering students must have completed three years of pre-osteopathic training. Most applicants have already received baccalaureate degrees in the sciences. The curriculum today is basically the same as most medical schools, but with more emphasis on the basic sciences, additional courses in osteopathic theories and methods, and the rural clinic program. After graduation, the physician serves a one-year internship in an accredited hospital and must also pass state and national medical boards in order to become licensed. That's a long ways from Dad's internship, which included jumping right in to deliver babies and take out tonsils, the first week on the job.

Today osteopathy has become accepted throughout the country, and every state offers unlimited licensing to Doctors of Osteopathy. Colleges of osteopathic medicine are graduating many students. In fact the nation has approximately 55,000 fully licensed osteopathic physicians practicing all kinds of modern medicine, including the holistic, hands-on approach to diagnosing and treating illness and injury. They look, not only at the immediate problem, but also at the whole body and all it's systems working together. Nearly one in five medical students today are training to be an osteopathic physician. They can choose any specialty, prescribe drugs, perform surgeries, and practice medicine anywhere in the United States. DO's are trained to look at the whole person from their first days of medical school, which means they see each person as more than just a collection of organ systems and body parts that may become injured or diseased.

The majority of most osteopathic medical school graduates choose careers in primary care and they have a special focus on providing care in rural and urban underserved areas. In addition to studying all of the typical subjects you would expect student physicians to master, osteopathic medical students take approximately 200 additional hours of training in the art of osteopathic manipulative medicine. This system of hands-on techniques helps alleviate pain, restores motion, supports the body's natural functions, and influences the body's structure to help it function more efficiently.

When I was getting my degree in biology in college, I was always taught that structure is related to function in the plant and animal world. This is very true of human beings also. Their structure influences function. So, if there is a problem in one part of the body's structure, function in that area, and possibly in other areas, will be affected also. The human body has an innate ability to heal itself, and manipulative techniques are aimed at reducing or even eliminating the impediments to proper structure and function, so the self-healing mechanism can assume its role in restoring a person to health.

Dad was always up on the latest advances in medicine and manipulation because he was always reading the current medical journals and attending continuing education courses around the country. There weren't many questions I had for him that he could not answer. It would be nice if he were here today to guide me through all the material in this book so I could spell all the names and places right, get the correct dates on things, and the correct twists on all the stories.

Chapter 39

A Tribute to My Dad – August 10, 2004

(I read this tribute at Dad's funeral in August 2004)

"My Dad" was a very special guy. I don't really know why, but I never referred to him as just DAD, I always said "my Dad".

He was "My Dad" but most of all he belonged to everyone in the community. Many times I felt like I never got to spend time with him, but the past few years have been different. We have had great times of sharing together as he and Carolyn have spent much time in our home because of illnesses and surgeries.

It was a privilege for me to grow up in the loving community of Unionville where my father was the beloved doctor to so many people for over 60 years.

Doc belonged to the whole community, including all of Putnam and Sullivan Counties, and I learned this early in life.

He delivered over 3,500 babies, and in some families that included three generation. He treated five generations for several families.

The doctor's household had no problem with teenagers monopolizing the telephone. Long before adolescence set in, I knew I had to keep my conversations brief. I also learned very young how to take a message, including the caller's name and number, the nature of their complaint, and any general information like TPR (temperature, pulse and respiration).

Teachers seemed to have an unshakable belief that I would be extraordinarily healthy. If I missed school, the teacher would say, "You a doctor's daughter, was sick?" Actually, nobody gets sick as often as doctors families because, no matter what the epidemic raging, Dad was busy sticking his face into infected throats, being breathed on by feverish patients, and coming home exhausted and bearing the day's invisible harvest of germs. If anything was 'going around" it was sure to "go around" our house.

But when we got sick, the treatment was usually a "do-it-yourself" procedure, mostly because Dad was never home. He had a lot of medical textbooks with articles illustrating in detailed color photographs, a victim's appearance. Mom would get my disease tagged, read about it in the book and call Dad to bring home the right medicine.

This may surprise you but during a serious illness it is an unwritten rule that a physician does not treat his own family nor does he charge a colleague for medical services. This automatically made our family the least sought-after patients on the face of this germ-ridden earth.

Yet much as every doctor hates to be called to another doctor's house, even more, because of the reflection on his skill, does he hate seeing someone else called instead. Years of professional relationships could hang while the debate on who to call went on. The usual result was that no doctor was called.

Everyday, the past few years patients would call the Judd residence, which also served as the medical office and they would hear, "Helloooooo, pardon me, I couldn't hear you!!!" The voice on the phone didn't belong to a receptionist, but to the doctor himself. At 87 years old he was the oldest practicing doctor in the state and maybe the country. If you needed surgery or had a heart attack, he would send you to one of the younger doctors in town but if it was the flu, a sore throat, a minor injury, poison ivy or bee stings, you could just take a seat in the living room and soon you would hear "Who's next?"

After he retired from his clinic and saw patients in his home, he didn't take Medicare or insurance. The charges ranged from $10 to $20 for a visit, depending on what services were required. The front door was unlocked and the patients just walked in and took a seat in the living room. They came from southern Iowa, Putnam, Sullivan, Mercer and Adair Counties in Missouri, and even as far away as Kansas City, because he was the only doctor they had ever known.

Dad always had a story to tell and everyone from teens to his old buddies at the coffee shop every morning at 8:00 enjoyed a good joke on a regular basis. He never forgot a punch line.

As others have said, he worked all the time. That was his life, day and night. My mother worked hard along with him in their first years of marriage, and after she had me to take care of, she spent many days and nights alone while he was taking care of others.

In his last few years, his wife, Carolyn, has been there taking care of many things, from the house, the meals, and Dad while he still worked everyday.

This past year, they have spent much time in our home, and it has been good. It was difficult watching Dad struggle to be healthy enough to be in his home, for truly he was not happy to be away from Unionville for any amount of time and his goal was always to get well enough to "go home".

Most of you know all these things about him already, but I will now share a little of the past six weeks in our home

After he fell and broke three ribs, he couldn't cough (and you know he needed to do that often), so soon he was developing pneumonia. We got out the antibiotics and I even gave him one of his "magic shots" but his old heart just needed more help. He ended up in intensive care in the hospital in Lee's Summit before coming back to our home. Either Carolyn, my husband, Ron, or I were with him 24 hours a day and we had many visitors and family help. Our children were there spending nights at Grandpa's bedside to give us a little time to sleep. **Shirlee** and **Richard Ryals** spent the night with him to help us also, and because they had been friends for years and he was the doctor for their large family.

Now, I want to tell you about some of the special times during these last weeks.

He spent much time singing his cute little songs, quoting the poetry which he memorized early in life and when things got real tough he's quote the 23rd Psalm. He was able to see almost all his grandchildren and great grandchildren and talk to them about life.

He prayed out loud a lot and he especially loved my husband's prayers. They were so soothing to him and he asked for them often. The day before he died he could hardly get enough breath to speak but he said to Ron, Pray...........short.

He was always doctoring others. Our Pastor, **Fred Allen**, stopped by for a visit, and Dad discovered that he had the shingles. Dad immediately gave him a shot and medicine to clear up his shingles.

Our dear friends adult granddaughter had a bad sinus infection and we set up the treating table, wheeled him to the head of the table and with his strong arms he gave her the treatment she needed to get better. When he couldn't get enough leverage to move her back he started to stand up (to which I protested) and he said just grab the back of my pants and hold on so I won't fall over.

Ron stretched out on the bed in our room a few days ago and Dad looked over at him and asked, "Do you need your back worked on?"

When we came up to Unionville for **Don Herrick's** memorial service, he worried the whole time that we had been in a car wreck. Ron put him in the wheel chair and took him to the garage to see that the car was all right when we got back. He was much relieved and proceeded to bow his head and gave Masonic Last Rites to the car. He never mentioned 'the wreck' again.

Many people have told me in the past few days that Dad was the only doctor they ever had and for Father's Day this year we got him the personalized license plates that lovingly says "UVL DOC".

I know that in the coming days and months I will have lots of questions that only my Dad could answer. I hope that some of you can help me answer some of these questions.

My memory will be of a father who was kind and didn't want to hurt or disappoint anyone and I will always know that he loved me unconditionally.

Part VI

Memories of the Times

Chapter 40
The Photo Gallery

Powersville, Missouri High School 1935

Warren Spears, Illinois   Calvin Shad, South Dakota Charles Judd, Missouri
College roommates 1939

Dr. Judd and Dr. Shad in 1999 at Mount Rushmore

Catherine Isabelle (Isa) Judd 1944. Charles Judd's mother

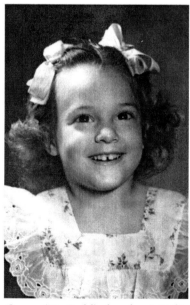

Serece (Dr. Judd's daughter) 1948

Dr. Judd, head nurse Bessie Runciman and office manager Wilma Cullom

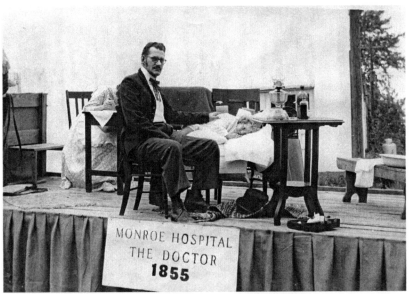

Unionville Centennial Parade: representation of 1855 doctor's home visit by
Dr. Charles Judd

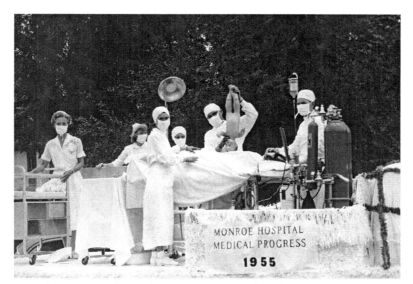

Unionville Centennial Parade: representation of modern hospital by Dr. L.W. McDonald and nurses

Ruth and Charles Judd 1965

Doc and Bill Davis in 1958 at the Lake of the Ozarks, Osage Beach, Missouri

Dr. Robert McCalment & Virginia. Dr. "Bob" was a dentist in Unionville with offices in both the Monroe Hospital and later the Monroe Clinic.

Charles Judd with brother, Howard Judd and Grandkids, Daniel, Matthew and Suzanne in 1980. The occasion was Dr. Judd's 40th Anniversary open house celebrating his years of medical practice in the area.

Dr. Judd with grandkids in 1987 in Lee's Summit, Missouri Daniel, Suzanne, and Matthew.

Dr. Judd with daughter, Serece, in 1987

Doc with Avis and Bill Davis

Cousins, Mildred Hodkins and Charles Judd 1998

Dr. Judd with E'Laine and Don Herrick. The Herricks owned and operated
Herrick's Rexall Drug Store in Unionville for 47 years.

Doc with sister Ruth Moss in Sun City, AZ 1988

Grandpa Doc with Matt Lewis in 1998. Matt is an Elvis Impersonator with
Legends in Concert in Las Vegas.

Serece and Ron Baker 2000

Ruth Magee, Danny Peto and Charles Judd at the Memorial Day Service in
Unionville 2003.

Nephew James B Judd and Doc Thanksgiving 2000

Doc with grandson Dan Lewis. Dan is a Chiropractor in Lee's Summit, Missouri

Great Grandpa Doc with Matt's son, Xander, 2002

Xander with Grandma Serece 2006

Doc and his high school buddy, Jim Cozad, enjoying breakfast together in Kansas City in 2002

Fishing buddies, Jim Molan and Doc, with a really big catch

Great Grandpa with Dan's son, Quinton Judd Lewis, 1996

Great Grand Children of Dr. Charles L. Judd
Back row: Xander and Chloe Lewis (children of Matt), Trevon Lewis (son of
Dan)
Front row: Quinton Lewis (son of Dan) Brooke Baker (daughter of Lance) and
Kyle Baker (son of Vaughn)

Serece Judd Baker, always a Unionville High School Midgets Fan.

Chapter 41
Dirt Roads

What's mainly wrong with society today is that too many Dirt Roads have been paved.

There's not a problem in America today, crime, drugs, education, divorce, delinquency that wouldn't be remedied, if we just had more Dirt Roads, because Dirt Roads give character.

People that live at the end of Dirt Roads learn early on that life is a bumpy ride.

That it can jar you right down to your teeth sometimes, but it's worth it, if at the end is home…a loving spouse, happy kids and a dog.

We wouldn't have near the trouble with our educational system if our kids got their exercise walking a Dirt Road with other kids, from whom they learn how to get along.

There was less crime in our streets before they were paved.

Criminals didn't walk two dusty miles to rob or rape, if they knew they'd be welcomed by 5 barking dogs and a double barrel shotgun.

And there were no drive by shootings.

Our values were better when our roads were worse!

People did not worship their cars more than their kids, and motorists were more courteous, they didn't tailgate by riding the bumper or the guy in front would choke you with dust and bust your windshield with rocks.

Dirt Roads taught patience.

Dirt Roads were environmentally friendly, you didn't hop in your car for a quart of milk you walked to the barn for your milk.

For your mail, you walked to the mail box.

What if it rained and the Dirt Road got washed out? That was the best part, then you stayed home and had some family time, roasted marshmallows and popped popcorn and pony rode on Daddy's shoulders and learned how to make prettier quilts than anybody.

At the end of Dirt Roads, you soon learned that bad words tasted like soap.

Most paved roads lead to trouble, Dirt Roads more likely lead to a fishing creek or a swimming hole.

At the end of a Dirt Road, the only time we even locked our car was in August, because if we didn't some neighbor would fill it with too much zuccihini.

At the end of a Dirt Road, there was always extra springtime income, from when city dudes would get stuck, you'd have to hitch up a team and pull them out.

Usually you got a dollar…always you got a new friend…t the end of a Dirt Road!

By Paul Harvey

Chapter 42
Thanks for the Memories

Long ago and far away, in a land that time forgot,
Before the days of Dylan, or the dawn of Camelot.
There lived a race of innocents, and they were you and me,

For Ike was in the White House in that land where we were born,
Where navels were for oranges, and Peyton Place was porn.

We learned to gut a muffler, we washed our hair at dawn,
We spread our crinolines to dry in circles on the lawn.

We longed for love and romance, and waited for our Prince,
And Eddie Fisher married Liz, and no one's seen him since.

We danced to 'Little Darlin,' and sang to 'Stagger Lee'
And cried for Buddy Holly in the Land That Made Me, Me.

Only girls wore earrings then, and 3 was one too many,
And only boys wore flat-top cuts, except for Jean McKinney.

And only in our wildest dreams did we expect to see
A boy named George with Lipstick, in the Land That Made Me, Me.

We fell for Frankie Avalon, Annette was oh, so nice,

And when they made a movie, they never made it twice.

We did have a Star Trek Five, or Psycho Two and Three,
Or Rocky-Rambo Twenty in the Land That Made Me, Me.

Miss Kitty had a heart of gold, and Chester had a limp,
And Reagan was a Democrat whose co-star was a chimp.

We had a Mr. Wizard, but not a Mr. T,
And Oprah couldn't talk, yet, in the Land That Made Me, Me.

We had our chare of heroes, we never thought they'd go,
At least not Bobby Darin, or Marilyn Monroe.

For youth was still eternal, and life was yet to be,
And Elvis was forever in the Land That Made Me, Me.

We'd never seen the rock band that was Grateful to be Dead,
And Airplanes weren't named Jefferson, and Zeppelins were not
Led…

And Beatles live in gardens then, and Monkees lived in trees,
Madonna was a virgin in the Land That Made Me, Me.

We'd never heard of microwaves, or telephone in cars,
And babies might be bottle-fed, but they were grown in jars.

And pumping iron got wrinkles out, and 'gay' meant fancy-free,
And dorms were never coed in the Land That Made Me, Me.

We hadn't seen enough of jets to talk about the lag,
And microchips were what was left at the bottom of the bag.

And Hardware was a box of nails, and bytes came from a flea,
And rocket ships were fiction in the Land That Made Me, Me.

Buicks came with portholes, and side shows came with freaks,

And bathing suits came big enough to cover both your cheeks.

And Coke came just in bottles, and skirts below the knee,
And Castro came to power near the Land That Made Me, Me.

We had no Crest with Fluoride, we had no Hill Street Blues,
We had no patterned pantyhose or Lipton herbal tea
Or prime-time ads for condoms in the Land That Made Me, Me.

There were no golden arches, no Perrier to chill,
And fish were not called Wanda, and cats were not called Bill.

And middle-aged was 35 and old was forty-three
And ancient were our parents in the Land That Made Me, Me.

But all things have a season, or so we've heard them say,
And now instead of Maybelline, we swear by Retin-A.

They send us invitations to join AARP,
We've come a long way, baby, from the Land That Made Me, Me.

So now we face a brave new world in slightly larger jeans,
And wonder why they're using smaller print in magazines.

And we tell our children's children of the way it used to be,
Long ago and far away in the Land That Made Me, Me.

As Bob Hope always said

"Thanks for the Memories"

You Will Be Remembered

You will be remembered when the flowers
bloom in spring

And in the summertime remembered in the fun
that summer brings

You will be remembered when fall brings
leaves of gold

In the wintertime remembered in the stories
that are told

And you will be remembered each day right
from the start

For the memories that we once shared live
forever in my heart.

Printed in the United States
217941BV00001B/3/P